ISLAM
IN OUR
BACKYARD

A novel argument

ISLAM
IN OUR
BACKYARD

A novel argument

TONY PAYNE

✿ **MATTHIAS MEDIA**

Islam in our Backyard
© Matthias Media, 2002

Distributed in the United Kingdom by:
The Good Book Company
Published in the United Kingdom by:
The Good Book Company
Tel: 0845 225 0880
email: admin@thegoodbook.co.uk
website: www.thegoodbook.co.uk

ISBN 1 876326 48 4

Cover design and typesetting by Joy Lankshear Design Pty Ltd
Printed in Denmark.

ACKNOWLEDGEMENTS

MY THANKS GOES TO the many people whose conversations, feedback and ideas contributed to the development of this book. In particular, my thanks to Mike Raiter for kindly allowing me to adapt material of his that ended up in chapters 2 and 4. I am also very grateful to Phillip Jensen, Kirsty Birkett, Greg Clarke, Ian Carmichael, Nader Mikhaiel, James Payne, Julie Rhodes, Fashid and Massy Baradaran, Megan Churches, Bruce Hall and Sam Green, for taking the time to read the manuscript in draft form and make many useful suggestions. And finally a great debt is owed to my wife, Alison, who not only read the manuscript and made many helpful comments, but who provided the constant love and encouragement which makes completing a project like this possible.

Dedication

This book is for Michael next door, whose name is not really Michael and who doesn't really live next door. 'Michael', and my conversation with him, are fictions formed from the dust of conversations over many years with neighbours, friends and complete strangers.

1

EARLY ON THE MORNING of September 11, 2001, two hijacked passenger jets, bearing 157 passengers and crew between them, rammed into the Twin Towers of the World Trade Centre in New York City.

The force of the explosions did not initially destroy the towers, which were built to withstand the horizontal impact of a large commercial aircraft. It was the fire that killed the buildings. The fire, fuelled by 91,000 litres of aviation fluid, and a forest's worth of office paper, reached temperatures in excess of 800 degrees centigrade. At these temperatures, the steel core of the buildings, and the steel members that supported the concrete floors, began to melt and buckle. Eventually, they collapsed under the massive load above, bringing a sudden catastrophic force to bear on the floors beneath, which were never designed to carry such a load. From this point on, the implosion of the buildings was inevitable, as each new collapsing floor added to the enormous downward force.

At 10:05 am, the north tower of the World Trade Centre, collapsed; the south tower followed at 10:28 am. Approximately 3000 office workers, firemen and policemen lost their lives.

I woke up on that morning to the red blinking lights of the clock-radio, and to the sombre tones of the news announcer. We stumbled downstairs and watched the images being repeated with ghastly regularity on the TV.

I walked out into the back yard. I wanted to see that the world was still there.

It was a clear, dry spring morning, bathed in bright, blue-tinged Australian light. The grass in the vacant block next door, the debris piled in the corner of our yard, the trampoline sitting at a probably unsafe angle near the back door—it was all still there. The clarity of it almost hurt the eyes.

A plane roared overhead, looming out of the block of red-brick flats, on its approach to the East-West runway at Kingsford-Smith. The sound it made was a shock.

I noticed Michael, our neighbour from across the back lane, packing something in the boot of his car. He stopped and looked up at the plane, as I did, and caught my eye.

"You heard what happened?" he said.

"Yes, unbelievable", I said.

"They reckon that it was Muslim fundamentalists", Michael said. There was a pause. "Don't know much about Muslims, but I don't trust them. Any of them."

I was surprised at the hardness in his voice. I was just as surprised at the mention of religion. Following the great Australian tradition, it wasn't something we ever talked about. In all our back lane chats over the previous 18 months, the topic of religion had entered the conversation only once, and only briefly, before making a rapid exit.

It was after my son had asked Michael's boy, Connor, whether he wanted to go to Sunday School. We were leaning against his verandah, in the way that men do when they talk with each other, both facing out. I had asked Michael what he thought of Christianity. He had frowned and said nothing for about 10 seconds, and I thought that I had offended him, or that he was about to break into a tirade and was trying to hold himself back.

Finally he said, "Religion's a personal thing. I think people's faith is something for them". And after a pause, "My mum sent me to the local Methodist Sunday School for a while, when I was 7. But I don't know whether I want my kids to hear just one religious point of view. Maybe they need a Sunday School where they get taught values and the spiritual side of life, but without it being any one religion. I mean they all teach the same values deep down."

"Well you could send him to the Ba'hai", I suggested with just a hint of sarcasm. "That's basically what they teach. Although I'm not sure their Sunday Schools are bursting at the seams."

"Yeah, well that's because they're a bunch of weirdos", said Michael, laughing.

I was about to follow up with a jovial "well what does that make you", when Michael's daughter Kelly called out from the back verandah. "I'm off now Dad. Back later tonight. Bye."

The joviality left Michael's face immediately. "Off where?" he shouted at the now vacant verandah.

But there was no answer, except the bang of the front door in the distance.

Michael attempted a half-smile. "Maybe I should've sent her to Sunday School."

"She giving you trouble?" I asked.

"Not really. She's a good kid. But I just don't like who she's hanging around with at the moment."

And so the conversation moved into one of those 'young people of today' modes, and the question of Sunday School and religion was left behind.

Until today, when Michael had mentioned Islam, as we stood together on the morning of the tragedy, hands in pockets, kicking around the gravel in the back lane, trying to find something meaningful to say.

"So what do you know about Islam?" I asked him.

"Not much. They worship Allah, don't they? They keep saying it's a religion of peace, but look at the Middle-East. I mean, I'm not a racist, but what about those gang rapes in Bankstown? And my sister-in-law who works for the Department of Community Services says that they systematically rip off the welfare system. In her area they're about 10% of the population, but they make 40% of the claims."

I was surprised to say the least. My fairly easy-going tolerant neighbour was turning into a red-neck racist before my eyes. It was probably the wrong thing to do, but I decided to play devil's advocate.

"But Michael, you once told that me you thought that all religions were much the same deep down."

A troubled look clouded his face for a moment. "Did I? I don't know. Maybe the Muslims I'm talking about aren't true Muslims. You know, fanatics and fundamentalists... But you're the religious one, what do you think?"

"Well, I don't know a lot about Islam either. One obscure fact I know, which I find fascinating, is that the Qur'an denies that Jesus was ever crucified. Somehow he was whisked away before the deed was done."

There was a longish pause. It was one thing for religion to make a brief foray into our back lane, but I wasn't sure Michael wanted it to hang around for too long.

But then he said, "Seriously? Is that what they say?"

"I'm pretty sure it is. I couldn't quote the Qur'an chapter and verse for you or anything, but I could check it out."

Another silence.

"What else do they teach?"

"Well, I only know in general terms. The five pillars of Islam, believing that Allah is the only God, and that Muhammad is his prophet. That sort of stuff. I've always meant to read more about it, but haven't gotten round to it."

"Look, if you do, let me know what you find out. I wouldn't mind reading something myself. But anyway, I'd better keep going."

In the weeks that followed, as my reading on Islam turned into the idea of a short book about Islam, I kept thinking about Michael. It was really for the Michaels I knew that I wanted to write. I not only wanted to fill in the gaps in people's basic knowledge about Islam; I wanted to explore the problems that Islam posed for the Practical Secularist. Because that's what Michael was, although he never would have given it such a label.

Practical Secularists are close cousins to the much rarer Theoretical Secularists. A Theoretical Secularist is committed, at an intellectual level, to 'secularism'. He believes that this world and this age (Latin, *saeculum*) are all that exists, and that the consolations and false dreams of religion should have no place in a modern society. In the stadium where the Theoretical Secularist plays, the roof is always closed. There is nothing and no-one upstairs. It's a closed system. There is not—and cannot be—any outside authority or 'god' to tell us what to do, or how to live together in society.

And so the Theoretical Secularist wants the church to stay well out of politics, and in fact out of life in general. If the deluded wish to continue to practise religion within the privacy of their homes, or within the hallowed walls of their antique buildings, that is their business. But believers must not be allowed to impose their morality on the rest of us. They should keep their superstitions to themselves. And if there comes a point where these religious beliefs transgress the laws and values that we as a secular society have come to hold dear, then the believers must adapt or suffer the consequences. The Theoretical Secularist tolerates religion, as one might tolerate people who believe they were abducted by aliens. "I regard religion as a disease born of fear and as a source of untold misery to the human race", wrote Bertrand Russell, one of the grand-daddies of modern Theoretical Secularism.

Michael would never say such a thing. It would be rude, and a little too hard-edged for his taste. He is not at all 'religious' himself, but he would not criticise someone who was. He may even have a vague sense of 'spirituality' in his quieter moments, and wonder whether there is indeed some 'god' or 'spiritual force' that animates the universe.

Yet for all practical purposes, Michael is still a secularist (a 'Practical Secularist'). The world he lives in is a secular, godless world. Despite superficial differences, all religions are much the same, and probably have a core of truth in them somewhere (something to do with peace and love and being kind to one another). They are something of an embarrassment in the modern world, a throwback to a simpler age. They belong in private where they cannot do too much harm.

But now some people claiming to act in the name of their religion had done a great deal of harm. Someone had forgotten to tell them that religion was a private matter, and shouldn't be allowed in the public arena.

It seemed to me that in the face of a militant Islam, the idea that religion is fundamentally private and not political, and that religions are all much the same, simply could not continue to stand. In fact, the more I thought about it, the more worried I became that unless our society could find a better basis on which to build than Practical (or Theoretical) Secularism, we were in big trouble.

With these thoughts in my head, I ran into Michael again one afternoon, as our boys rode their scooters in the lane.

"Listen, Michael, I've got an unusual request to make."

"Sure, what is it?"

"I've been doing a fair bit of reading about Islam, and I've decided to write something about it. And in fact, the reader that I'm aiming at is someone exactly like you."

"Not sure what you mean."

"Someone who isn't really religious, who doesn't know much about Islam, is disturbed about recent events, and is having a bit of a post-September 11 think about religion."

"Well, yes, I guess that's me."

"So my request is: Will you help me write the book? I'd like to show you what I'm writing as I go, and get your reactions and comments. I'd show you a draft of some stuff, and we could chat about it. It would help me enormously, and I thought you might find it interesting too."

Michael looked a little stunned. But with a half-smile he said, "Yeah, that might be good. I wouldn't mind that. But do I get half the royalties?"

"Sure", I said. "I'll also put your name on the cover, and send a copy to the local Al-Qaeda network."

Michael laughed, and Connor, right on cue, came careering out of the carport and slammed into his leg. Michael howled first in shock, and then in exaggerated mock pain. He teetered stiffly like a tree, and fell over.

2

IT TOOK ME SIX WEEKS, putting other projects aside, to put together even a first instalment to show Michael. Even then I wasn't happy with it.

I thought the place to start would be to summarise the basic things that all Muslims believe, but this was a much harder task than I imagined. Islam is big, and complex. I guess any religion that's been around for 1400 years and boasts around one sixth of the world's population for adherents is bound to be. There's a multitude of groups, sub-groups, sects, schools, traditions and ethnic variations.

What's more, there's no one source or authority that you can go to for a definite answer. Islam has no pope, and no central institution or 'church' as such. There's no officially sanctioned 'Office for the Deciding What Islam Really Teaches'.

Islam does have a holy book, the Qur'an, that is deemed to be the supreme authority, but even this doesn't help a great deal. All the different Islamic sects and groupings claim the Qur'an as their foundation, and the lofty and enigmatic nature of much that the Qur'an contains provides ample opportunity for different emphases and interpretations.

And just to make a tricky task even trickier, in the weeks following September 11, everybody was rushing to put forward their take on Islam. The Internet was aflame with wild rants having the basic theme of 'I Always Knew That Muslims Were A Bunch of Blood-Thirsty Towel-Heads'. And the media was full of impassioned pleas urging us to realise that 'Islam Is A Tolerant Religion Of Peace Being Misrepresented By A Tiny Minority Of Crazed Fundamentalists'. What was the truth, what was spin, and what was uninformed prejudice?

As I tried to sort through it all, and the pile of books and articles grew ever higher on my desk, it occurred to me that, as a Christian, I knew how some Muslims must be feeling. I often felt misrepresented and offended by the portrayal of Christians in the media. They always seemed to get us wrong—or at least, to get me wrong, and most of the Christians I knew. They either portray us as lunatic-fringe fundamentalists at war with the modern world, or else as woolly-minded fools pathetically attempting to accommodate their faith to a world that no longer believes it. And I guess the reason they so often get us wrong is that they don't really understand us; they don't know what makes us tick, and what is genuinely important to us. It's simpler and easier in the end to go with the stereotypes, and to frame a good conflict story around them.

I didn't want to do that with Islam. If I was going to end up saying anything meaningful about Islam, I wanted to understand it first, and represent it fairly. I realised that I would need to show my drafts not only to Michael, but also to some Muslims.

It was after six weeks, then, that I finally had something that I wasn't ashamed to run past Michael. It was my attempted summary of the bed-rock Islamic beliefs that virtually all Muslims, as far as I could tell, would believe; a kind of 'Apostles Creed' of Islam.

I dropped it over to Michael on Sunday afternoon.

"So this is chapter 1?" he said.

"Well, the guts of chapter 1 at least", I said. "It's still pretty rough in places. I haven't worked out a snappy intro, or even a conclusion, but it's got the basic content. It's a start."

"OK. Fine. What do you want me to do again?"

"Just read it, and tell me how it strikes you. Scribble on it if you think something doesn't make sense, or sounds wrong. Write down anything you can think of that would help. And don't hold back. I've got a thick skin."

"All right. I'll start on it tonight."

"Great. Let me know when you've finished, and we can talk."

WHAT DO MUSLIMS BELIEVE?

Any religion of 1 billion adherents, spanning a history of more than a millennia, will contain within it enormous diversity of belief and practice. We must bear this in mind as we attempt to outline the essential beliefs of Islam. What we are attempting to do is distil and explain, in a very simple way, a whole complex of ideas, teachings, traditions and practices that have shifted and developed over a period of 1400 years.

With that qualification, let us proceed.

Muhammad and the Qur'an

Although we might say that Islam began with Muhammad, Muslims of course would say that it began with Allah. For Muslims, Muhammad is not only the Messenger of Allah, the one through whom the revelation of the Qur'an came; he is the model Muslim. According to Muslim tradition,

Muhammad underwent practically every possible human experience in his various roles as teacher, merchant, family man, and political and social leader. Consequently, in behaviour and conduct he is the ideal standard for every Muslim to follow. In some countries, such as Pakistan, any abuse or expression of disrespect towards Muhammad is a criminal offence, punishable by death.

The Qur'an itself says little about the life of Muhammad, and there is not much independent historical information about him apart from the *hadiths*—a collection of the deeds and sayings of Muhammad, compiled some 200 years after his death. (The *hadith* literature is very important in Islam, for reasons that will become clear below).

According to the tradition, Muhammad received his first revelations while meditating in a cave outside Mecca. The angel Gabriel appeared to him and commanded him to recite what he heard (Qur'an = 'recitation'). Muhammad was uncertain at first whether it was really the angel of God who was talking to him, or some evil spirit or *jinn*. Yet encouraged by his wife, Khadijah, he persisted with his meditations, and the revelations continued. Eventually, after Muhammad's death, they were compiled into one book (the Qur'an), although there is not a great deal known about the process by which the compilation took place.

After the initial revelations in Mecca, Muhammad began to gather a small band of believers around him, who were convinced that Muhammad was indeed God's Messenger, the last and greatest of the prophets. Muhammad's message of strict monotheism, and his strong critique of the idolatry and pagan practices of his contemporaries in Mecca, led to persecution by the authorities. Eventually, in 622, he was forced to leave Mecca and move north to Medina. At Medina, Muhammad was welcomed and his teachings accepted, and he soon came to power as the city's political and religious ruler.

As his power base grew in Medina, he conducted successful raids on the surrounding areas, and eliminated opposition to him within Medina—in particular the Jews. It was in Medina that the laws and practices of an Islamic society were first drafted and enacted; it became the model for the ideal Islamic state. Muhammad continued to receive revelations in Medina, in particular relating to the problems and challenges of constructing and ruling a theocratic society—that is, a society in which God rules through his representative ruler and a God-given law.

Eventually, Muhammad returned in military triumph to Mecca, and negotiated a surrender of the ruling Quraysh (who had once persecuted him). By the end of his life, he had conquered almost the entire Arabian peninsula, and united the disparate tribes and factions within the one brotherhood of Islam.

The trajectory of Muhammad's own life—from persecuted minority to theocratic ruler, from Mecca to Medina—is very important to Islam. According to traditional Islamic teaching, the world is divided into two spheres: the sphere of Islam, in which Islam rules, and the sphere of War, in which there is still struggle and conflict between Islam and unbelievers. The ideal path for all Islamic communities is to transform the sphere of War into the sphere of Islam; to move from being a struggling minority to establishing an Islamic state; in other words, to move from Mecca to Medina.

This dynamic is also very important in understanding the Qur'an itself. It is generally accepted by Islamic scholars that the 'softer' sayings of the Qur'an regarding the importance of religious tolerance, and the need to live in peace and harmony with unbelievers, stem from Muhammad's Meccan period, in which he himself was a persecuted religious minority. The 'harder' more triumphalist parts of the Qur'an, with its exhortations to fight the unbelievers and kill them if necessary, are said to come from the Medinan period. Muslim scholar, Shaykh Fadhlalla Haeri writes:

> The nature of the Qur'anic message in Mecca was to do with faith, belief, trust in and submission to Allah, selflessly, generously living this life in preparation for the next. In the Medina phase, however, the revealed message and prophetic actions dealt mostly with matters of community, family and social life, trade, war, law and all the other regulatory foundations required for a civilized society.[1]

Thus, those Muslims who find themselves living as minorities in non-Muslim states, need to take to heart the 'Meccan' parts of the Qur'an and live peaceably with their neighbours. Conversely, the 'Medinan' teaching applies to those Muslims who find themselves in the ascendancy in a community, and offers instruction in the establishment of a society based on Islamic law.

Just to make things even more interesting, it is not at all apparent from the Qur'an itself which sayings are from Mecca and which from Medina. The Qur'an contains 114 *suras* (or chapters), arranged not chronologically or according to subject matter but simply from longest to shortest. This is where the *hadiths* (the traditional collection of Muhammad's deeds and sayings) become so important. It is through the *hadiths* that Islamic scholars seek to determine the context and application of particular parts of the Qur'an. The *hadiths* are like a lens through which the Qur'an is read and interpreted, because they represent how Muhammad himself understood and lived out the principles of the Qur'an. In practice, then, the *hadiths* are of equal authority with the Qur'an.

Unfortunately, it's very hard to tell how authentic the *hadith* material really is. The stories and sayings were handed down and spread orally for some 200 years before they were sorted, sifted and written down, most famously by two men, al-Bukhari and al-Muslim. Not surprisingly, non-Islamic scholars tend to be very sceptical about the reliability of the *hadiths*, not just because of the time-span involved, but because many of the stories seem either to contradict one another, or to go against the Qur'an itself.

There is also considerable dispute between different branches of Islam about the authenticity of different *hadiths*. A whole field of Islamic scholarship has developed over the centuries to delve into this question, and to seek to establish which *hadiths* are most trustworthy, and which should be rejected. There are some Muslims who reject all the *hadiths*.

All the same, it is fair to say that most Muslims believe that some portion of the *hadith* literature is true and accurate, and provides access to the life of the Prophet himself. The *hadiths* are thus indispensable for interpreting the Qur'an itself.

This brings us to our next question. Having understood something of Muhammad, and how the Qur'an (and Islam) came to be, what did Muhammad teach? What was the message that Gabriel instructed him to recite?

Muhammad's message
Allah
'Allah' is simply the Arabic word for 'the god', and it refers in Islamic teaching to the one true God of all the world. When Muhammad came forth from the cave outside Mecca, it was not with the news that he had discovered a new 'god'. He claimed that it was the God of Abraham, Isaac, Ishmael, Israel, David and Jesus who had spoken to him through an angel, and had dictated to him the pure and final revelation of his will for the world.

Islam claims, then, to be the legitimate and final successor to Judaism and Christianity, and to worship the same God. Much of what Islam teaches about Allah is thus quite recognisable to Jews and Christians—and indeed to secular Westerners, whose culture has been built on Judaeo-Christian foundations. In Islam, Allah is seen as the creator and judge of all the world. In his purity, holiness and power, he is in charge of all things, and orders all events in the world. He is just, and will render to every person on judgement day according to what they have done.

However, Allah is also portrayed repeatedly in the Qur'an as a compassionate and merciful God, who is also ready to forgive sinful humans who submit to his will. Even so, it would be a mistake to equate this characteristic of Allah with the personal, loving 'Heavenly Father' of Christian belief. Islam rejects the idea that Allah is 'personal' in this sense, or that humans can have a 'relationship' with him. In Islam, Allah is transcendent, unapproachable and ultimately unknowable. He is to be feared and obeyed, rather than befriended.

Unity

Few words in the Islamic vocabulary are more important than the word 'unity'. Muhammad strongly affirmed the oneness of God, who alone is to be worshipped. He was thus a trenchant critic of the prevailing polytheism and idolatry of his time, and also of the Christian belief in the trinity.

Based on the oneness of Allah, Islam also affirms the oneness of Muslims. While they may be divided into different sects and groups, scattered across the globe from Hyderabad to the Outer Hebrides, there is one *ummah*, or community, of all Muslims. To varying degrees, all Muslims share an identity of being part of a global brotherhood. Conservative Muslims hope that one day there will be one world, a world united in submission to Allah.

This sense of 'oneness' lies deep within the structures of Islamic belief. Jesus may have said, "Render to Caesar the things that are Caesar's, and to God the things that are God's" (Matthew 22:21), but Muhammad made no such distinction between the civil and the religious. There is no 'church' or 'religious institution' as such in Islam—no organization, separate from the state, that co-ordinates and regulates the faith of believers.

In fact, the absence of a 'church/state' distinction within Islam is one of the key factors in understanding the conflicts that arise, both within Islamic countries and in the West. The ideological heartbeat of Islam is always towards a unified, Islamic state, in which the will of Allah regulates all the affairs of life. There is no privatised sphere of religion in Islam.

The universalism of Islam is therefore based on the universalism of Allah himself, and of Muhammad's revelation of him. In this sense, Islam is a religion 'programmed to win'.[2] And in its early centuries, following the death of Muhammad, winning is largely what it did. The rapid expansion of Islam throughout the Middle-East, Western Asia, North Africa, India and into Europe is one of the stunning phenomena of history.

However, for this very reason, long decline of Islamic power at the hands of the West, accelerating over the past 200 years, has been hard for Muslims to bear. The frustration and hostility of many conservative Muslims towards the West has its roots in a deep sense of historical and religious outrage. Muslims cannot help but feel that the 'wrong side' has become the supreme power in the world, and is exerting its influence politically and culturally even within Islamic countries.

Submission and law

Islam means 'submission', and a Muslim is 'one who submits', although this word does not capture the full meaning of 'Islam'. It is related to the word 'salaam', the Islamic greeting of peace. Islam is submitting oneself to him with whom peace is made. Then, through this life of submission to the will of God, the one who surrenders to God finds peace both here in this world and in the world to come. Indeed, Muslim scholar, Ameer Ali, argues that the concepts of peace and salvation are more fundamental to the meaning of 'Islam' than submission. He writes,

> The word (Islam) does not imply, as is commonly
> supposed, absolute submission to God's will, but
> means, on the contrary, *striving after righteousness*.[3]

Keeping the law (or *shari'ah*) is at the heart of the life of
submission. Submission to God means submission to his
law, and his law is comprehensive. It is intended to govern
each and every part of a person's life, from the cradle to the
grave, and deals with everything from political, economic
and social affairs, to how one should pray, fast, and even
sneeze and drink water.

The *shari'ah* is built on four foundations or 'roots' in
descending priority. The Qur'an itself is the supreme
authority, but there are many aspects of life about which it
says very little, especially by way of detailed instruction.
The *hadiths* are the second root of Islamic law. The practice,
for example, of Muslim men wearing beards stems not
from a command in the Qur'an but from the *hadiths*, which
record that Muhammad wore such a beard.

If some aspect of life is not covered by either the Qur'an
or the *hadiths*, the consensus and common practice of the
Muslim community establishes the law that is to be
followed. This consensus, or *ijma*, may of course vary from
time to time, and place to place, and much of the variation
in Islamic practice, historically and geographically, can be
traced to particular local practices and patterns being incor-
porated into the *ijma* of the Islamic community. This is why,
for example, some Islamic communities practice female
circumcision, while others reject it.

The final root of *shari'ah* is *qiyas* or analogical reasoning.

If a matter cannot be established from the Qur'an, *hadiths* or *ijma,* then reasoning can be used to deduce what should be done. For example, the Qur'an only specifically prohibits alcohol made from grapes or the date-palm. Using *qiyas,* Islamic jurists argue that since the principle behind the prohibition is the avoidance of intoxication, then other alcoholic drinks (such as vodka) are also forbidden.

The practice of Islam

While there is variation in the content and practice of *shari'ah* throughout the world, all Muslims would acknowledge the 'five pillars' on which obedience to Allah is built.

First, Muslims confess the oneness of Allah, and the finality of his prophet. Muslims believe that every prophet, from Adam to Jesus, was a prophet of Islam, each one proclaiming the same message and applying it to their own time and place.

Second, Islam requires of its followers that they pray five times a day at fixed hours of prayer. These particular hours of prayer are not set down in the Qur'an, but Muslims base this practice on what is believed to have been the custom of the prophet (recorded in the *hadiths*). Together, rich and poor, in unison bow down with their faces towards Mecca, expressing their united submission to God. The 'prayers' that are offered are not usually personal petitions or requests, such as to beg Allah's help in solving some life problem. They consist of the recitation, in a strict form and with set liturgical movements, of verses from the Qur'an.

The other three pillars are: fasting from sunrise to

sunset during the month of Ramadan; giving (at least) two and a half percent of one's income to the poor; and making a pilgrimage at least once in one's life to the *Ka'ba*, the home of the sacred black rock, in the city of Mecca.

Islam is a religion of good works, whereby the eternal happiness or misery of an individual is determined largely by the amassing of meritorious works while here on earth. Nonetheless God is utterly sovereign and totally free to do whatever he wills. A Muslim's life of righteousness does not make God his debtor. Every Muslim, ultimately, must trust himself to God's mercy. In his sovereign mercy he may acquit the most wretched infidel and, by the same token, be free to withhold eternal pleasures from the most ardent follower of the prophet.

Conclusion

This is a much-abbreviated and simplified picture of the essential structures of Islamic belief, and the practices which spring from it. All the same, I hope it is an accurate picture, which represents those things which Muslims, by and large, hold in common.

Our next step, however, is to attempt to understand the diversity of modern Islam. How is it that many Muslims praise and support the actions of Osama bin Laden, while others label him a fanatic who distorts the true nature of Islam?

1 Shaykh Fadhalla Haeri, *The Elements of Islam,* Shaftesbury: Element Books, 1993, p.16.
2 A phrase coined by Malise Ruthven in his book, *Islam in the World*, Harmondsworth: Penguin, 2000.
3 Ameer Ali, *The Spirit of Islam.* Karachi: Afro-Asia Publishers, 1984, p138.

3

WE SAT ON MICHAEL'S DECK, at a suite of teak outdoor furniture that had been vandalised by their dog, and looked out over the backyard. It was Monday afternoon, just over a week since I'd given Michael chapter 1.

Michael didn't work Monday afternoons. It had something to do with that being one of the days Julie could get work at the hospital (she was trying to keep her hand in at physiotherapy), and Julie's mother who normally looked after Dylan on Thursdays couldn't do it on Mondays because that was her bingo day, and so Michael organized a long shift on Fridays so that he could finish early on Mondays and pick up Dylan from Martha's, whom Julie knew from school, and who took Dylan for a few hours in the morning.

Michael's was a pretty normal modern family, in other words. Julie was his second wife, and he was determined to try to make it work this time around. The only time he had ever mentioned his first marriage was to say to me one day, "We were young, we were stupid, and we didn't have a clue what we were doing. Eventually, Rachel just cleared off." Kelly was from the first marriage, and lived with them. His two boys, Connor and Dylan, were from the second marriage, and Michael looked forward to having Monday afternoons with Dylan, and with Connor when he came home from school.

Dylan was busy digging up the lawn in the corner near the

cubby house while Michael and I sat on the deck. Michael had obviously decided that a little buffalo-grass was a sacrifice worth making for some peace.

We settled back with some coffee. Michael untucked his old t-shirt from his faded jeans, and leaned back in his chair. He was a big man, with brown eyes and dark hair, with just the hint of gray above the ears.

"So what did you think?" I finally asked, after we had avoided talking for a while.

"Yeah, it was good. Very interesting."

There was a pause. "OK, great", I said, "I'll just head off and write chapter 2 then".

"Good, thanks for coming. Have it ready for me tomorrow", said Michael.

"Right. No problems."

We laughed, just a little awkwardly.

I tried again. "So why don't we start with any bits that didn't make sense."

"OK." He started leafing through the draft. "There were some little things, and some bigger things... Start with a little thing: You wrote about the Qur'an and interpreting it and so on. My grandmother, who was a full-on Methodist, used to read the Bible every day, and she always wanted to read it to me when I came over on the weekends. If she was a devout Muslim, she'd be reading the Qur'an in the same way, right? That's their Bible."

"Well, yes and no", I replied. "The Qur'an is their 'Bible'—you're right about that. But from what I could gather, it's not something the average Muslim would sit down and read every day for inspiration. It's more of a holy artefact, almost; an object of intense veneration and respect, but quite hard to read and understand for yourself. It's written in 7th century Arabic for a start, and has only been translated into English fairly recently.

"Most Muslims would rely on the teachings they were brought up with, the traditions and practices of their particular community, the instruction given to them by their local religious leaders, the mullahs and imams. They wouldn't see it as their prerogative to open up the Qur'an and work out what it means, even if they were able to do so."

"OK, the mullahs and imams. But you said somewhere that there is no 'church' in Islam", said Michael. "But I've scribbled down here: 'What about mosques? Aren't they like churches?'"

"Well, again I suppose I could say yes and no. The mosque is a gathering place for prayers and for instruction. In this sense, it's similar to the 'church buildings' of Christendom. It's the religious headquarters in a particular community. But what I was getting at with saying there was no 'church' in Islam is that there is not the split that we might be familiar with in the West between 'church' and 'state'. There is no 'religious institution' which rules Islam or speaks for Islam. And in the ideal Islamic state there is no separation into two realms or powers: the religious realm and the secular realm of politics and society. It's all one. In this sense, it's a very 'this-worldly religion'. I mean, it believes in heaven and hell and judgement and so on—but it seeks to become triumphant in this world, and to establish the rule of Islam here and now, politically and socially. The laws of an Islamic society will be shaped and directed by Islam—no alcohol, blasphemy laws, a special tax on non-Muslims, laws against a Muslim converting to Christianity, and so on."

Michael looked thoughtful. "Well, where does that leave Muslims in democratic societies?"

"With something of a dilemma", I replied. "The idea of an open, tolerant free expression of ideas, in which there is freedom of religion, seems quite foreign to the structures of Islamic thought. Because Islam is a universalistic religion—there is only one God and Muhammad is his prophet—the idea that you would willingly tolerate alternative beliefs is rather foreign. And so in countries where Islam rules, there is rarely anything we would associate with tolerance or freedom of expression or democracy. One statistic I didn't include in the chapter was that of the 46 member nations of the International Islamic Conference, only one has a properly democratic government (that's Turkey). I mean, look at Libya or Iraq or Yemen or Sudan or Pakistan or even Indonesia and Malaysia for that matter. These are what we would call repressive governments. Democracy doesn't exist, or is compromised. There is active persecution of religious minorities. It's not pretty.

"And this is what gives the Muslim in modern Western society something of a dilemma", I went on. "At one level, he appreciates the freedom of an open, democratic society. Sometimes, he has fled from his Muslim homeland because of its repressive conditions. And yet, if he is to be true to his faith, he would wish his new-found nation also to become an Islamic state, in an ideal future."

Michael sat forward in his chair. "So you mean, if Australia, for argument's sake, became 40 or 50% Muslim, they'd try to make it into an Islamic state?"

"Quite possibly."

"Well, we should kick them all out, then."

As Michael said this, he suddenly looked at me, with a

mixture of fright and surprise. Did I just say that, his eyes were saying? I really am a reasonable sort of guy, not a racist, his look said. I've got nothing against Muslims coming to Australia and doing their thing within our free multicultural society. But what if their thing involves being opposed to multiculturalism? I may regard religion as a private matter, and therefore wish to grant them the right to free expression of their faith—but what if, to them, religion is *not* private? What if the free expression of their faith eventually meant a political campaign to dismantle the very democratic structures that allowed them freedom in the first place?

I'm not sure Michael's look of unease represented quite as many rhetorical questions as that. In fact, I'm sure it didn't. He was just startled to find himself sounding like a racist.

I well understood Michael's sense of unease. In deciding to write a book like this, I didn't want to tiptoe around the truth about Islam. I didn't want to 'spin' it as a warm, cuddly, non-aggressive religion if that was not, in fact, what it was. Then again, I didn't want to end up writing a rabid apology for the White Australia Policy, and then be doused in chardonnay and set on fire by the local chapter of 'Free Thinkers for a Multicultural Australia'.

But there was no avoiding the problem. There seemed to be something deeply incompatible between Islam and what we call 'democracy'. I had read quite a lot about this, and the more I read, the more disturbing it was.

For example, the respected Harvard Islamist Bernard Lewis suggests that the historical incompatibility of Islam and democracy is in part due to the lack in Islamic thought of the concept of a corporate legal entity, a body or council that had legitimate power to acquire property, enter into contracts, and so on. The proliferation of councils, synods, diets and assemblies of all kinds that flourished in Christendom had no counterpart in Islamic history. And it was these corporate entities that laid the foundation for the idea of a parliament, and of a representative democracy. By contrast, says Lewis, "almost all aspects of Muslim government have an intensely personal character. In principle, at least, there is no state, but only a ruler; no court, but only a judge. There is not even a *city* with defined powers, limits and functions, but only an assemblage of neighbourhoods, mostly defined by family, tribal, ethnic or religious criteria, and governed by officials, usually military, appointed by the sovereign".

As Lewis goes on to argue, the legislative power of a Western democratic parliament is also out of step with the tenor of Islam, in that the Islamic state is in principle a theocracy—that is, a state ruled by God, according to his law. Whatever rules or laws an Islamic ruler might establish, they must be seen as elaborations or interpretations of the only valid law—that revealed by God through revelation. Lewis concludes:

> Without legislative or any other kind of corporate bodies, there was no need for any principle of representation or any procedure for choosing representatives. There was no occasion for collective decision, and no need therefore for any procedure for achieving and expressing it, other than consensus. Such central issues of Western political development as the conduct of elections and the definition and extension of the franchise therefore had no place in Islamic political evolution.

Not surprisingly, in view of these differences, the history of the Islamic states is one of almost unrelieved autocracy. The Muslim subject owed obedience to a legitimate Muslim ruler as a religious duty. That is to say, disobedience was a sin as well as a crime. (Bernard Lewis, "Islam and Liberal Democracy", *The Atlantic Monthly*, Feb 1993)

Like many commentators, Lewis's solution to this dilemma is to suggest that for Islamic countries to embrace democracy, and to forge a place for themselves in the modern world, they will have to develop a new expression of their faith. Islam will have to evolve in some way, and bring those elements to the fore (and he points to a few hints and historical precedents) which can encompass modern ideas of democracy.

Question is: Would it still be Islam? Can it evolve without compromising its essential nature? This is the question to which more moderate 'secular' Muslims say Yes, and more conservative Muslims say No. That's the trouble with a perfect, timeless, divine revelation, I guess. If it's in need of updating, is it really perfect any more?

Which brings me back to Michael, who was frowning and contemplating the mess Dylan was making of the lawn.

I was wondering where we'd go next. I didn't really want to get into a discussion about immigration policy at this stage—either in the book, or with Michael. So I did what I normally do when faced with such dilemmas: nodded in a non-committal way, and changed the subject.

"Any other comments?" I asked.

Michael said nothing for a while.

"No, not really", he said finally. "I mean, what you've written is good, and it bothers me a bit. But I don't know what to do with it at the moment."

"That's fine", I said. "We're just getting started. Where do you think we should go next?"

"Well, I liked the way your chapter finished—promising that we were going to look further at Osama bin Laden, and at why some Muslims support him. Because I'd still like to understand where the fundamentalists fit in... And women. That's the other thing. What's the Muslim view of women?"

This last comment surprised me. Michael was a modern male who had come to terms with feminism, and lived in an uneasy détente with it. He was no chauvinist, but I hadn't picked him as a campaigner for the cause of women in Muslim countries.

As it turned out, he had reasons for wanting to know.

4

Hi Michael,

Dropped in to give you the next bit, but you were out. It's taken me a bit longer than I expected, but hey—what else is new? I'm also a bit worried that I've gotten carried away in parts, and that it's too strong. But then, as I read back over it, it seems true to me. I don't know.

Also, I haven't got to the 'women in Islam' bit yet, but I will soon.

Let me know when you're ready to talk again.

T.

THE MANY FACES OF ISLAM

The question that has been on many people's minds since September 11 is a simple one: Are Osama bin Laden and the Taliban genuine, representative Muslims, or a small lunatic fringe?

This is an important question for obvious reasons. If what the Taliban is fighting for is what most Muslims also want, then the West is in for a long and bitter conflict with a powerful and numerous enemy. Was September 11 the awakening of the sleeping Islamic giant? Was it the first shot of World War III, fought out between the West and Islam? Or was it merely the action of deranged and criminal extremists?

This question has been debated endlessly in the media, and over backyard fences, since September 11. There have been plenty of voices reassuring us that Islam is, in reality, a religion of peace, and that all true Muslims would be opposed to such acts of terror. Yet it did not escape anyone's attention that this was a very politically expedient message, used in part to build a broad-based coalition to oppose the Taliban. It was the message we all wanted to hear, but was it the truth?

Before we can answer this question with any sort of accuracy or fairness, we must familiarise ourselves with the enormous *diversity* of Islam. Westerners tend to lump all Muslims together, and refer to 'Islam' as a single, monolithic entity, as if all (or even most) Muslims throughout the world believed and did the same things. This could not be further from the truth. There are profound differences between the Shi'ite Muslims of Iran, the Wahhabi Muslims of Saudi Arabia, the Sunni Muslims of Indonesia and the nominal, barely theistic Muslims of Kosovo, to name but some.

Let's seek to understand something of this diversity, before we try to locate where Osama bin Laden and his like fit in.

Two broad streams

Perhaps the best way to understand the breadth of Islam is to identify two broad streams, each with its own branches and sub-branches. These two streams are the Sunnis and the Shi'ites.

The rivalry and enmity between these two groupings has a very long history, going back to the very beginnings of Islam. It was basically a dispute about who should succeed Muhammad after his death in 632.

Initially, Muhammad's closest companion, Abu Bakr, became his successor (or *Caliph*). Abu Bakr died just two years later, and was succeeded by Umar. After Umar's assassination, Uthman took control and during his caliphate (644-56) he determined the official text of the Qur'an, having ordered the burning of all other texts. He, too, met a bloody end, and was followed by Ali, Muhammad's cousin and son-in-law, who was pronounced Caliph in 656.

This is where the less-than-harmonious question of the succession erupted into war, and in one sense this is understandable given that the religion established by Muhammad was as much about politics and the state as it was about private devotion. Without going into the complex details of who conspired with whom, the result was that Ali was murdered, and his sons defeated in their attempts to be his successor. Muawiya, the ruler of Syria, became Caliph, and from that point most Muslims accepted the legitimacy of his rule, and of his successors. These Muslims became known as *Sunnis* (that is, those who base their faith on *al sunna,* the way of the Prophet).

The supporters of Ali, however, rejected the legitimacy of all the Caliphs after the first four (Abu Bakr,

Umar, Uthman, Ali), whom they considered were the only ones 'rightly guided'. They became known as *shi'a* (or shi'ites), 'the party of Ali'. The enmity that has marked the Sunni/Shi'a rivalry throughout history continues today, where there are often violent clashes between the two groups in countries where they live together.

How do Sunnis and Shi'ites differ in belief? In many respects, their beliefs are the same. Both believe in the five pillars of Islam, although differences have evolved in how they practise some of the rituals. One significant difference stems from their divergent interpretations of Muslim history.

Shi'ites believe that leadership in the Muslim community is vested in the Imam, who is the final authoritative interpreter of God's will as it is expressed in *shari'ah* law.

In a sense, the Christian counterpart of the Shi'ites is Roman Catholicism, in which the institutional leaders have the final say, with the Imam as a kind of pope. The Islamic revolution in Iran was a Shi'ite revolution, and the Ayatollahs of that country possess enormous influence and authority.

For Sunnis, religious authority does not reside so much in one individual, but in the consensus (*ijma*) of the collective judgment of the community, based on the Qur'an and the *hadiths*. In a sense, the Sunnis are more like Protestants, who give greater weight to the authority of the ancient texts. At present, about 90% of the world's Muslims are Sunni.

Four overlays

The Sunni and the Shi'ites are the two dominant streams of

Islam, although a variety of sub-branches and smaller groups also exist. Floating over the top of these broad streams are four 'overlays' or tendencies which will influence how particular Muslims within those streams will practise Islam.

For example, Islam has its mystics—the Sufis—who find the severe, transcendent Allah of classical Islam too distant and unapproachable. The Sufis (who might be Sunni or Shi'ite) seek a closer, more intimate relationship with Allah through fasting, other ascetic practices, spiritual exercises and ecstatic worship. The famous dance of the 'Whirling Dervishes' is a sufi ceremony.

Islam also has its modern Secularists, the counterpart to liberal Christians and progressive Jews, who want to update Islam for the twenty-first century, and forge a synthesis between modern ideas and the traditions of Islam. These secular Muslims are largely found in the Western countries to which they have immigrated, and again may be either Sunni or Shi'ite by tradition. They typically wish to maintain something of their cultural and ethnic identity as Muslims, and yet also wish to distance themselves from aspects of traditional Islam which they regard as outmoded, distasteful or no longer culturally relevant, especially in the West.

However, lest we think that the modernist, secularist Muslims are dominant, because we tend to see more of them in the West and hear them in the media, we need to recognize that a vast number of the world's Muslims are quite conservative and orthodox in doctrine and practice. They do not see any need to update the Islamic faith, to improve it, or to render it more acceptable to the modern world. Saudi Arabia, for example, is dominated by the Wahhabis, a conservative school within Sunni Islam, which follows a very literal interpretation and application of the Qur'an. The Taliban (or 'students'), who had their origins in the conservative Islamic schools of Pakistan, are also Sunnis. The conservative Islamic movement in Iran, however, is Shi'ite.

The fourth overlay we need to bear in mind is what we might call 'folk Islam'. There are many Muslims in the world today, in a wide variety of countries and cultures, whose practice of Islam is fused with local beliefs, traditions and superstitions. These might include the veneration of Muhammad and other Islamic heroes and saints by wearing protective amulets, visiting their shrines, and praying to Allah in their name.

This sketch of the diversity of Islam is brief and to some extent simplistic. One additional point that must be made to fill out the picture is that many Muslims are nominal believers. Islam is for them a badge of cultural identity, and gives a certain shape to their lives (depending on the society they live in) but they do not hold passionately to the beliefs, nor practise the required religious duties with any fervour (if at all).

Westerners tend to believe that all Muslims in countries like Iran or Afghanistan are religious fanatics, who leap up and down in mass demonstrations and burn American flags. This is largely a media construct, and does not represent the reality. In Iran, for example, the populace are far more pro–American than the conservative religious leaders would like to admit. Indeed, there is currently a power–struggle taking place between the reform-minded government of Khattami, and the Shi'ite clerics who still hold considerable power following the 1979 revolution.

We would do well not to accept the media stereotypes too quickly.

The roots of militancy in Islam

The question remains: Within the broad spectrum of Islamic belief and practice, where do terrorist groups such as Al-Qaeda fit in? Are they merely the sharp end of what has always been an aggressive, militaristic religion? Or have they hijacked 'peaceful Islam' for their own political ends?

Again to answer this question we must sketch in some historical background. Many Westerners don't know their own history very well, let alone that of other civilisations and societies. The history of Islam has been, except for perhaps the last 300 years, largely one of triumph and glory. Muhammad's conquest of most of the Arabian peninsula within his lifetime was the start of an extraordinary march of victory that was to last nearly a thousand years.

By the end of the century following Muhammad's death, Islam had conquered not only all of Arabia, but had pressed into Armenia, Syria, Palestine, Persia, North Africa (including Egypt), Spain, Turkey and India.

We must be clear about the fact that this expansion did not proceed by preaching or persuasion, but by military force. From the beginning, the concept of *jihad* was central to Islam's self-identity, and to its methods. It is historically unsustainable to suggest otherwise. Modern apologists for

Islam sometimes say that *jihad* is really about an inward struggle against evil, but this is a distinction that, historically speaking, Islam has never accepted. The war against evil and unbelief is carried on against both the inner demons and those outside. There is no distinction. It is the consistent and unambiguous teaching of the Qur'an (especially in the Medinan period) and the *hadith*, that Muhammad's followers were to follow his example in furthering the cause of Allah's true religion by waging war against the unbelievers. To get a feel for this strand of Islamic teaching, here is a representative selection of quotations from the Qur'an and the *hadith*:

> O Apostle! Rouse the believers to the fight. If there are twenty amongst you, patient and persevering, they will vanquish two hundred. If a hundred, they will vanquish a thousand of the unbelievers, for these are a people without understanding. (Qur'an 8:65)
>
> Fighting is prescribed for you, and ye dislike it. But it is possible that ye dislike a thing which is good for you, and that ye love a thing which is bad for you. But God knoweth, and ye know not. (Qur'an 2:216,217)
>
> Say to the unbelievers, if (now) they desist (from unbelief), their past would be forgiven them, but if they persist, the punishment of those before them is already (a matter of warning for them). And fight them on until there is no more tumult or oppression, and there prevail justice and faith in God altogether and everywhere. (Qur'an 8:38-39)
>
> But when the forbidden months are past, then fight and slay the pagans wherever ye find them, and

seize them, beleaguer them, and lie in wait for them in every stratagem (of war). But if they repent, and establish regular prayers and practice regular charity, then open the way for them. For God is oft-forgiving, most merciful. If one among the pagans asks thee for asylum, grant it to him, so that he may hear the Word of God; and then escort him to where he can be secure. That is because they are men without knowledge. (Qur'an 9:5-6)

Fight those who believe not in God nor the last day, nor hold that forbidden which hath been forbidden by God and His Apostle, nor acknowledge the religion of truth, (even if they are) of the people of the Book, until they pay the *jizya* with willing submission, and feel themselves subdued. (Qur'an 9:29-31)

A man came to Muhammad and said, "Instruct me as to such a deed as equals Jihad (in reward)." He replied, "I do not find such a deed." Then he added, "Can you, while the Muslim fighter is in the battlefield, enter your mosque to perform prayers without cease and fast and never break your fast?" The man said, "But who can do that?" (Hadith of Bukhari, 4:44)

Muhammad said, "I have been ordered to fight with the people till they say, 'None has the right to be worshiped but Allah,' and whoever says, 'None has the right to be worshiped by Allah', his life and property will be saved by me except for Islamic law, and his accounts will be with Allah (either to punish him or to forgive him.)" (Hadith of Bukhari 4:196)

There is no question that violent means and military

expansionism have been integral to Islam from the very beginning. Indeed, given the unity that Islam sees between religion and the state, it could hardly be otherwise. The expansion of Islam *is* the expansion of the Islamic state.

One can only conclude that Western apologists who downplay the military expansionism of Islam either have not read or do not believe what the Qur'an and the *hadith* say on these matters. After the death of Muhammad, the expansion of Islam continued apace. Muslim scholar Azim Nanji summarizes it thus:

> By the year 712, just eighty years after the death of Muhammad, Muslim armies had begun to take control of the Iberian Peninsula in the west and the Indus River valley and Central Asia in the East... This situation was brought about by several waves of armed conquest, the first of which began shortly after the Hijra [that is, Muhammad's move from Mecca to Medina]. From his base in Medina, the Prophet had triumphed over his opponents in Mecca and the Hijaz, and extended his influence to Arab tribes throughout the Arabian Peninsula. Those who did not convert from among Arab groups and continued to oppose and fight with Muslims, including Jews and Christians, were expelled or defeated in battle. After Muhammad's death, the caliphs...and their representatives succeeded both in consolidating the religious iden-tity of the community and harnessing tribal ener-gies by authorizing raids into Syria and Iraq... Soon thereafter Arab Muslim forces inflicted defeats on Byzantine and Persian armies opened

the way of the conquest of Syria, Mesopotamia, western Iran and Egypt between 634 and 644. From the ancient city of Damascus and the newly created garrison towns of Ira (Basra and Kufa) and Egypt (Fustat), a third wave of conquests emanated that brought Arab Muslim armies into eastern Iran, Armenia, Libya and Tunisia by 670.[1]

The career of Muhammad and the early expansion of Islam is a story of military aggression, violence and political assassination. And the teachings of the Qur'an and the hadith not only describe some of these events, but give divine approval to them. From its outset, in its foundational holy texts, and throughout the vast bulk of its history, Islam has been universalistic in ambition and warlike in methodology.

This is reflected in the incredulity of devout Muslims towards the claims of secular Muslims or Western observers who want to say that Islam is fundamentally peaceful and tolerant in nature. The Ayatollah Khomeini responded to these claims thus:

> Islam makes it incumbent on all adult males, provided they are not disabled and incapacitated, to prepare themselves for the conquest of countries so that the writ of Islam is obeyed in every country in the world.
>
> But those who study Islamic Holy War will understand why Islam wants to conquer the whole world...Those who know nothing of Islam pretend that Islam counsels against war. Those [who say this] are witless. Islam says: Kill all the unbelievers just as they would kill you all! Does this mean that Muslims

should sit back until they are devoured by [the unbe-lievers]? Islam says, Kill them, put them to the sword and scatter [their armies]. Does this mean sitting until [non-Muslims] overcome us? Islam says: Kill in the service of Allah those who may want to kill you! Does this mean that we should surrender to the enemy? Islam says: Whatever good there is exists thanks to the sword and in the shadow of the sword! People cannot be made obedient except with the sword! The sword is the key to Paradise, which can be opened only for Holy Warriors! There are hundreds of other [Qur'anic] psalms and Hadiths urging Muslims to value war and to fight. Does all that mean that Islam is a religion that prevents men from waging war? I spit upon those foolish souls who make such claims.[2]

In other words, to place the adjective 'militant' in front of Islam, as if there is an essential Islam that is not militant, is to misunderstand Islam. Theologically, philosophically, politically and historically, Islam is militant. It seeks to diminish the House of War and expand the House of Islam until there is only 'submission', that is, only Islam. Militancy and violence are bound up in the heart of Islam, in a way that they are not in say, Buddhism or Christianity.

Of course, throughout Muslim history, there have been those who have not embraced its military and expansionist tendencies. And there are many Muslims in the world today who have no desire to fight, to conquer nations, to take over the world, or to do any such thing. Many Muslims today feel quite positive towards the West, and would like to share in the freedom and prosperity they observe in Western nations. Many have emigrated to the

West for precisely this reason.

However, in doing so, they do not reflect the heart of Islam. In fact, it is this very tendency among Muslims—to admire the West and absorb its values and practices—that explains, in part, the rise of modern Islamic radicals and terrorism.

The roots of Islamic terrorism

So far, I have suggested that military expansionism and conquest are central to Islamic belief and history. Yet, of course, it has now been many centuries since Islam felt itself in the ascendancy. Beginning with the defeat of the Ottomans by Austria and Poland in the late 17th century, Islam has been in steady decline. Militarily, it has been defeated again and again, by Britain, by Napoleon and France, by Russia, by Italy, by Greece, culminating in the final defeat of the Ottoman Empire in the First World War. Over the past 300 years, the borders of Islam have been steadily beaten back.

For the religion 'programmed to win', this has been a bitter pill to swallow. The infidels have not only become militarily superior, but are more prosperous, more sophisticated and more dominant in nearly every field of human endeavour. The House of Islam is not just in retreat. It has become utterly dominated by the House of War.

Muslim reaction to this steady decline over the past three centuries has been varied. Some have argued that the growing superiority of the West represented a challenge to Islam to modernise, to move beyond its traditions and dogmas, and to absorb the best of what the West had to offer. Indeed, Muslim states have attempted in various ways to emulate Western practices and techniques, not always with success.

Others vehemently rejected this course, and argued that, on the contrary, what was needed was a return to the pure Islam of the 7th century, and that Islam's decline was a punishment from Allah for its slackness and apostasy.

Thus, the last 300 years has seen a succession of Islamic reform movements of various kinds, seeking to call Muslims back to the practice of their historic faith, and to resist the siren call of the West. One of the earliest and most significant of these was the Wahhabi movement, originating in the eighteenth century. Muhammad bin Abdul Wahhab was a native of northern Arabia who preached obedience to the letter of the Qur'an and the traditions. His goal was to purge Islam of the contaminations that were infecting it, whether practices borrowed from Christianity or introduced by the mystic Sufis. Wahhab found a patron in the tribal chief Muhammad bin Saud.

By the beginning of the nineteenth century the Wahhabis controlled most of what is now Saudi Arabia. Saudi Arabia, with its vast oil reserves, has been an enormously influential country in the promotion of conservative Islam. Thousands of Muslims from other nations have come to Saudi Arabia for employment. While little love may be lost between them and their proud, wealthy Saudi employers, these expatriate Muslims have seen the strict Islamic system at work. The *hajj*, or pilgrimage, also brings millions of Muslims to the Holy Places in Arabia where, again, they are brought under the influence of the conservative Islam of Saudi Arabia. Further, the petrodollars have enabled Arabia to export Islam, build mosques all over the world, promote evangelism (or *dawah*), and finance Muslim scholarship and theological colleges.

More moderate Islamic nations have seen more radical and conservative movements spring up in their midst, such as the Muslim Brethren of Egypt and the Jama'at-i-Islami in Pakistan. Such groups oppose the increasing influence of Western secularism in their nations. In particular, they oppose the willingness of their national leaders to have dealings with the United States which, largely because of its support of Israel, is seen as Islam's most potent enemy.

Until the rise of the Taliban, by far the most well-known expression (at least in the West) of this Islamic radicalism had been the Iranian revolution. Despite the support of the army, the police, the dreaded *savak* (secret police), and the backing of the West and other more moderate Islamic nations, the Shah of Iran could not withstand the conservative forces for change in the country. Under the all-pervasive influence of Ayatollah Khomeini, Iran established a twentieth-century Shi'ite Islamic state.

Islamic revivalism or radicalism moved even further to the right with the appearance of the Taliban in Afghanistan. The Taliban, or 'students', first appeared in 1994, emerging out of the Islamic schools of Pakistan. They were first appointed by the Pakistani government to serve as body-guards to a convoy trying to open up a trade route between Pakistan and Central Asia. With the assistance of former freedom fighters they went on to capture the southern city of Kandahar in 1994, and the capital, Kabul in 1996. Their aim was to establish the purest Islamic state in the world, banning music, television and pictures of living beings, and enforcing law and order through public hangings and amputations. At the time of writing, the Taliban seem to be on the verge of extinction in the US-led 'war against terrorism'.

In many respects, the radical Islamic reform movements have had as their goal not so much the conquering of the world for Islam, but resistance against the encroachment of Western power and influence—politically and culturally—into Islamic lands. Very often, the enemy that Islamic radicals despise most is the 'moderate' Muslim leader of their nation, who may be allowing Western ideals and practices to flourish within the country, and who co-operates with Western nations (such as the US) for political and economic purposes.

Accordingly, the terrorist acts directed against Western (especially US) targets are not an attempt to defeat or conquer America. They are largely an effort to drive American presence and influence out of the Islamic world. The ostensible cause of Osama bin Laden's fury was the presence of American troops within the holy lands of Arabia (a consequence of the Gulf War, and US cooperation with Saudi Arabia).

However, it is also a lashing out against the forces of modernism, globalization, and the relentless march of Western values and culture. For conservative Muslims, including the radicals, these forces are seen as being deadly to Islam, and to the integrity and identity of Islamic nations. Western secularists find this hard to understand. We tend not to realise how keenly our cultural imperialism is felt by orthodox believers in Islamic lands; how the seemingly irresistible march of Western culture is experienced as an oppressive and tyrannical imposition on cherished traditions, practices and beliefs.

The religious motivation of Islamic radicals is thus all of a piece with a desire to establish and maintain their ethnic and political identity. And since Islam draws no distinction between the religious and the political, it is a creed in which this potent mix of tribal pride, political frustration and religious zeal can bubble and foment.

In effect, then, the rise of radical Islamism, and its expression in acts of violence and terrorism, stem from two historical realities:

> Firstly, from the universalistic nature of Islam, and the doctrine of *jihad* that is intrinsically connected with this. Violent military means have always been central to the progress of Islam in the world, and it is simply dishonest to pretend otherwise. Moreover, this methodology is explicitly embraced and recommended in Islam's foundational documents. Theologically, historically and culturally, Islam has always been an aggressive, militarist religion.

> And secondly, from the long, steady decline of Islam at the hands of the West, and the consequent assault on Muslim identity and pride. When a proud, militant and once triumphant religion finds itself downtrodden and oppressed, it is to be expected that there will be resistance.

This is why both Ayatollah Khomeini and Osama bin Laden can appeal to the Muslim faithful to support them in their cause, and quote the Qur'an in doing so. They are not portraying anything that is not there; they are not distorting or misquoting. And accordingly, they do receive a great deal of support from Muslims around the world, who do resent the downtrodden state of Islam, and like to regard the West (and in particular the United States) as the cause of their woes.

Of course, the issue this leaves us with is: What are we going to do about it? What should our attitude be as Westerners to this form of Islamic militancy?

Logically, there would seem to be three options:

1. We can join it, as the true revelation of God in the world, and encourage all others (Muslims and non-Muslims) to do the same.

2. We can oppose it as misguided, wrong and harmful, and encourage all others (Muslims and non-Muslims) to do the same.

3. Or we can tolerate it as a valid form of religion, being sincerely practised by a large number of people, and do nothing to censure or oppose it.

1 (A. N. Nanji, *The Muslim Almanac*, Detroit: Gale Research, 1996)
2 Amir Taheri, pp 226-7 Holy Terror, London, 1987.

5

It was a week after I had dropped the latest instalment in to Michael, and time for another of our chats. I wandered across the lane and into Michael's backyard at around three. It was another perfect Autumn afternoon, the temperature hovering around 23, a gentle breeze blowing the occasional leaf from a tree. An afternoon more for golf than discussing manuscripts, I thought to myself.

I spotted Dylan in one of his favourite places—the narrow, earthy corridor between the garden shed and the fence—where he was in the middle of playing out a drama involving his collection of McDonald's Snoopy toys.

"Hey, Dylan, where's Dad?" I called out.

Dylan looked up at me, but said nothing.

It was then that I heard shouting coming from the house. There were two voices, a male and a female. I guessed that one was Michael, but the other didn't sound quite like Julie— which it shouldn't be anyway, since Julie was at work.

I hesitated. The time-honoured traditions of Australian neighbourliness said that I should immediately withdraw and later pretend to Michael that I hadn't heard anything, while sharing all the details with the other neighbours.

Unaccountably, I kept walking towards the house, and up the four wooden stairs to the deck. The argument was continuing, except that I could now distinguish three voices. One was definitely Michael, and another was Kelly, but the third—another male—I didn't recognize.

I stood on the deck, feeling awkward and yet captivated, trying to tell myself that I was trying to help. The voices were coming from the front of the house somewhere, across the family room, and down the hall towards the front door.

There was a sudden crescendo, and I heard Michael's voice, "Just get out! Just get the hell out of my house!"

Looking through the glass doors of the family and down the hall, I saw a figure stumble backwards out of one of the front rooms. It was the male whose voice I didn't recognize, a big teenage boy in oversized jeans and white shirt. He hit the wall hard on the other side of the hall and slumped down. Michael followed him out, and stood looking down at him.

His voice was angry, but faltering, "Look, just… just go. Go now."

It was like watching a drama on a very narrow stage: the boy slumped against the wall not moving; Michael, just visible in the doorway on the other side of the hall; Kelly now pushing past him and stooping over the boy, helping him up, the two of them stumbling towards the door.

"Kelly, get back in your room. Kelly!"

Michael was searching for the voice of command, but it wasn't working.

The front door opened, and Kelly and the boy left without saying anything. Michael was now framed in the hall, back to me, motionless, staring at the open front door.

The guilty realization hit me that Michael would turn around any moment now, and see me standing there on his deck, an uninvited spectator to his domestic drama. I turned quickly to head back down the steps and out of sight. Perhaps

I could pretend that I was just arriving and hadn't seen or heard anything.

As I turned, and took a quick stride towards the steps, I felt my left leg bump into something soft. I realized too late what it was, and let myself fall forward, twisting to one side and scooping my right arm round under my body to try to catch Dylan before he went down. His head thudded into the wooden decking with a noise that seemed impossibly loud. I tumbled over next to him, bringing down one of the teak chairs, and landing hard on my right hip.

Everything stopped. Dylan drew breath after the first long silent scream, and howled. Michael was already bounding through the family room, and out onto the deck.

Written on his face was the confusion and despair of an ordinary man trying to cope with the simultaneous onslaught of more emotions than he had experienced in the previous six months combined.

I scrambled to a sitting position as he went to Dylan.

"Oh, Dylan, little mate, are you all right?"

He picked him up and held him close.

I started to mumble something, "Look, Michael, I'm so sorry. I was just here on the deck and I turned round and didn't see the little guy and…"

But Michael wasn't listening, or didn't seem to be. He was just repeating, "Are you okay? Are you okay? Are you okay?" and rocking back and forward on his haunches, holding Dylan.

"Listen, I'm sorry about this", I went on. "Let's not worry about talking this afternoon. I'll… I'll catch you later, and we can take it up again next week maybe."

Michael looked up at me blankly, and registered my existence. "Yeah, whatever. Sure, that's fine."

"Is he okay, do you think?" I asked.

"Yeah, I think he'll be fine. They're pretty tough."

And he didn't say any more. He just kept rocking back and forth, holding the gradually quietening form of Dylan.

I hobbled down the steps, and back across the yard.

Dylan, as it turned out, was indeed fine. Apart from an egg-sized lump on the back of his head that went down after a few days, there was no damage—except to my reputation, which plummeted to a new low for some weeks. Whenever Dylan saw me coming, he would retreat to the space behind the shed and stay there until I was safely gone.

With Michael, there was thankfully no such intolerance of my presence. When I popped over the following day after work to check how Dylan was, he laughed it off, and made some diplomatic remarks about how kids take knocks all the time, and how it was just an accident.

In fact, it felt very much as if he were apologising to me, and not vice versa. Perhaps he had figured out that I must have heard and seen something of what had happened with Kelly.

In any case, when next Monday came, I found myself again enjoying the view from the teak chairs on Michael's deck, a coffee on the table beside me, and a backyard devoid for once of Dylan.

"Where's Dylan disappeared to?" I asked Michael when he sat down.

Michael looked at me deadpan. "He heard you were coming and refuses to come out from under his bed."

"You're kidding."

"No, seriously. He's terrified of you. If I even just happen to mention your name, he just starts screaming and throws himself on the floor."

"You are kidding."

Michael laughed. "He's over at Rohan's this afternoon, which means that it'll be their backyard that gets dug up, not ours."

I smiled and looked out over the grass to the treated-pine fort, with its garish paint-job, the fruit of many small hands with many pots of poster paint.

"So where do you want to start?" I asked.

Michael flicked through the pages. "Let me try and sort something out. In the first part of the chapter, you talk about the different kinds of ... streams, you call them, in Islam. How there are lots of different sorts of Muslims around, and we shouldn't lump them all together, right?"

"Yes, that's right."

"But towards the end of the chapter, when you were talking about militancy in Islam, you tended to talk about it as one thing. That seemed a bit inconsistent to me."

"Mmm, okay. I see what you mean. It's just that the radicals don't all fall into one of the streams. The Ayatollah Khomeini and the Iranian revolution—they were Shi'ites. Osama bin Laden and the Taliban—they're Sunnis. I guess you could say that you don't get many radical, violent Sufis; they tend to be more mystical and pious. And the modernizing secular Muslims, almost by definition, are not the violent radicals. But the vast majority of Muslims in the world are Sunnis, and the Shi'ites are the next biggest group. Between the two of them, they'd account for maybe 95% of the world's Muslims. And it's from within those two groups that the radicalism comes—but not that all Sunnis and Shi'ites are radicals. I suppose that's all as clear as mud."

"No that helps", said Michael. "What you're trying to say is that Islam, as a whole, has a history of war and violence, and that this goes right back to Muhammad, the Qur'an and…the other things, what are they again?"

"The hadith."

"Yeah, the hadith. But that in the 'big tent' of Islam today, there are some who want to be peaceloving and moderate, and some who don't."

"That's right", I responded. "And as with just about everything, politics and spin gets involved. So the moderate Muslim leaders try to argue that Islam is really all about peace and love, in order to ingratiate themselves with the West, for political and economic gain; and the more hardline Muslims argue that Islam involves fighting for the truth against the unbelievers, in order to build their constituency among the mass of conservative Muslims in countries like Iran or Afghanistan. I guess what I'm arguing is that for the 'peace-loving' Muslims to argue their case, they pretty much have to ignore large swathes of teaching in the Qur'an and the hadith, plus the historic practice of the Muslim community."

Michael looked thoughtful. "Yeah, that makes sense. But I thought I heard Cat Stevens on TV quote something from the Qur'an about peace and respect for other religions. Is there that sort of stuff in the Qur'an."

"Oh yes, there is. There are some quite respectful verses about the Christians and the Jews, and how they have nothing to fear from Islam. But the way Muslim scholars reconcile these with the more warlike verses is to point to the two main periods in Muhammad's life—the Meccan period (roughly

612–22) when he was leading a small persecuted minority in Mecca; and the period in Medina (from 622 onwards) when he was growing in military and political power. Basically, the softer sayings come from Meccan period, and the more aggressive and violent verses from the time when he had gained power in Medina."

"You mentioned that Mecca-Medina thing earlier. Maybe you should put it back into this chapter as well for thickheads like me."

I laughed. "Maybe I should. It's certainly a very important basic structure in Islamic thought. The shape of Muhammad's career—from Mecca to Medina—is the ideal path for the Islamic community; to pass from persecuted minority to pure Islamic state."

Michael put the chapter down in his lap, and stared into space. "So what you're saying is that bin Laden and Khomeini and the like are not hijacking Islam off into some distortion. They're calling for the faithful to return to their roots, and cast off the yoke of the oppressor."

"Something like that."

There was a silence.

"So religion for them is not a private thing?"

"Ah…no."

"Well there goes option number three then."

"Sorry?"

"Your three options at the end of the chapter." Michael counted them out on his fingers. "You suggested we basically had the choice to join 'em, oppose 'em or co-exist with 'em in a peaceful tolerance. Well my preference would definitely be number three. But that's only going to work if we all agree that religion is something basically private that you keep to yourself. I mean if your religion teaches that religion is public and should direct all of life, including the state, and you should keep struggling and fighting to win your state for Islam… Well how do you co-exist peacefully with that?"

"I think if you asked Christians and other minorities living in Muslim countries, they'd say that basically you can't."

"Well what do we do then? Lock them up? Throw them out of the country? Put quotas on how many we let in? Why don't we all just become members of the Ku Klux Klan and be done with it!"

Michael was getting quite animated by this time. I sipped my coffee while the idea of the Ku Klux Klan hung there. I don't know whether Michael had used the image deliberately. It was certainly calculated to press all my buttons. Or maybe he'd seen that episode of *The West Wing* where they suggested that the Taliban was to Islam as the Ku Klux Klan was to Christianity—which was very clever, but also very wrong. It would have been much more accurate to say that the Taliban was to Islam what Zionism was to Judaism; but then they never would have said that, or could have said that, Democrat politics being what they are.

I looked across at Michael.

"Well there were two other options."

He grunted. "Yes, well I didn't really like either of them."

"Why not?" I said with a raised eyebrow.

"Well, there's no way I'm going to be joining Islam. And given what you've written about it, I don't really want other people to either. But I also don't really want to oppose it either. I mean it just seems arrogant and intolerant to be going around saying, 'You're wrong!', especially about religion. Couldn't we have a fourth option? Something like a limited toleration of

Islam, where we allow them to exist and practise their religion, but only so long as they don't transgress certain norms of society."

"Not sure how that really helps you", I responded. "You're still saying to a Muslim person that certain aspects of their religion are 'morally unacceptable' in some way and will not be tolerated in our society. That seems pretty arrogant. Who are we to tell them that their religious practice transgresses our norms? Who says your norms are the right norms? You're still making a value judgement about their religious practice. It's just that you're trying to pick and choose which bits you do it on."

Michael looked thoughtful. "I see what you're saying. Option 4 tries to limit those things that you might declare 'wrong', as far as our society goes, but you're still making a call. You're still open to the charge of being arrogant, and passing judgement on someone's religion."

"So what's wrong with passing judgement on someone's religion?"

"Well…", Michael paused. "I was about to say that religion is a personal thing, but that doesn't work with Islam. We've been there, done that. I guess what I'd say is that religion is about belief and faith, not facts. And that you can't therefore prove it one way or the other, because it's a matter of personal belief. So you shouldn't pass judgement."

"So you'd say that it was wrong to pass judgement on someone's firmly held personal religious belief?"

"Yes, I guess I would."

I gave Michael a mischievous grin. "Well, that's what you've just done, isn't it? You've just passed judgement on all the world's conservative Christians and Muslims, because they all believe quite fervently that their beliefs are right, and that other religions are wrong. But since you say that it's wrong to pass judgement on other religions, then you're saying that all those Christians and Muslims are wrong to say that other religions are wrong. And so you've just passed judgement on them, and done the wrong thing."

Michael looked at me and didn't say anything. After a short pause he opened his mouth to say something, but before he could, what normally happens at interesting moments in conversation happened right on cue. His mobile rang.

"Sorry mate, I should get this."

He stood up and walked into the family room, and started to walk around, looking for all the world like he was talking to himself. His voice got steadily louder.

Then he burst out, "Jesus Christ, Kelly, what the hell were you thinking of?! Look, hang on a sec…"

Michael poked his head out the door. "Look, sorry about this. I have to go and sort this out…"

"That's fine. I'll just write something else and give it to you sometime. Maybe what we were just talking about at the end?"

"Yeah, fine. See ya."

And with that he was walking back through the family room and down the hall, talking animatedly and heading for the front door.

———

Later that night in my study, as I looked back over the notes I'd scribbled, and mulled over their significance, it occurred to me that the little book on Islam that I had been planning was taking an unexpected twist. The issue was becoming not

'What is Islam about?' or 'Is this a war with Islam?', but 'How does religion in general fit into modern Western society?' and 'Why do we find it so hard, in principle, to debate religious issues?'.

I strongly suspected that the answer lay in the course Western thought had taken over the past 200 years, but that was going to be no easy topic to deal with.

With too many ideas reverberating in my brain, I went to bed and tried, unsuccessfully, to sleep.

6

Dear Michael,

Not sure if this material should go in the book or not, but it seems the next logical step in our conversation, following on from where we got to the other afternoon.

There are two parts to it. The first is about the church v. state issue; that is, how the government should interact with religious belief.

The second part follows on from that, and is about religious belief in society as a whole, and the problem that Islam poses, in this respect, for modern Western thought.

Sorry that it's a bit long, but I hope you'll find it worth the effort.

Talk to you soon.

T.

PART 1: CHURCH AND STATE

So far, we have begun to gain an understanding of the main structures of Islamic belief and practice, to appreciate the diversity that exists, and to trace the range of factors that have given rise to modern Islamic radicalism and the violence of September 11.

The challenging question we have now come to is this: What is, or should be, the place of religious belief within human society?

It is a question with a long and bloody history. Should the state (in the form of the emperor, or caliph, or king or parliament) establish a particular mode of religious belief as compulsory and all-encompassing? Or should a plurality of views be accepted and tolerated? And if so, how far should that tolerance extend?

Or course, the particular form in which the question confronts us at present is especially difficult, because it deals with the place of Islam within modern Western societies. Should Islam be tolerated if it is itself intolerant? If the impulse of Islam is anti-democratic, what is its place within a democracy?

These are the questions many in the West are finding increasingly disturbing in the wake of Sept 11. They are questions that many Muslims have been struggling with for much of the past century.

Before we proceed to discuss these questions, and to see where that discussion might lead, one point of clarification is needed about the word 'state'. In talking about 'church' and 'state', or the attitude of 'the state' towards religion, the 'state' is the political organization or structure which is the basis of government for a country or nation (whether that is a monarchy or democratic republic or whatever). 'State' in this usage means something very similar to 'government', and that is how we will be using the word in the discussion that follows. However, as the Oxford Dictionary explains, 'state' has a number of other meanings, one of which is to refer to the whole nation, the body of people who occupy a particular territory, and who are united under a sovereign government of some kind or other. In this usage, 'state' is similar to 'country' or 'nation' or even 'society'. Because the relationship between the government and society as a whole (that is the 'state' and the 'state'!) is the very substance of what we're discussing, it might be useful to use different terms for each. And so we will use 'state' to refer to the government, and 'society' to refer to the body of people governed by them.

With that important little qualification, let us proceed.

The Islamic answer

As we have already noted above, the very idea of the 'church' and the 'state' (that is, government) being separate entities is foreign to the structures of Islamic thought. In a sense, there *is* no 'church' or 'state' in Islam; just the *ummah*, the community of Muslims, whose task is to establish God's just order throughout the world.

This order is comprehensive: it does not simply relate to private belief and behaviour, but to the structures and norms of society, to law and government. The vision of Muhammad was not for a church or religious community operating discretely within society, with its own authority structures and rule, and perhaps being a positive influence on the whole of society. His programme was to unite all

Arabs in one god-fearing society, built upon God's law, with God's prophet at its head—that is, an Islamic society and an Islamic state. His use of military force to fulfil this programme was quite consistent with his aims. His was not a private belief system, to be spread simply by persuasion and prayer; it was a programme for a new society, a new social order, in which injustice and idolatry would be done away with, and godliness would prevail.

The modern Islamic reformist, Mawlana Mawdudi, who founded the Jamaat-i-Islami movement, put it like this:

> Islam is not a religion in the sense of a hodge podge of some beliefs, prayers and rituals… It is a comprehensive system that tends to annihilate all tyrannical and evil systems in the world and enforce its own programme…in the interests of mankind.[1]

In these strong words, Mawdudi expresses something that Westerners often misunderstand about Islam. The great military jihads of Islam, beginning with Muhammad's own campaigns in the 7th century, were not so much attempts to gain more individual conversions at the point of the sword; they represented a programme to spread the just order of Islam throughout the world. The programme was to grow the House of Islam and to subjugate the House of War; to increase the boundaries within which the law of Allah (the shariah) regulated society.

Of course, individuals were caught up in this, and were faced with a moment of decision. For the People of the Book (that is, Jews and Christians) the choice was to convert to Islam or to become a kind of second-class citizen within the Islamic state (having to pay a special tax, and with reduced social and legal rights). The choice for all other conquered unbelievers was even more stark: convert, become a slave or die.

However, all this was quite consistent with the social worldview generated by Muhammad's revelations. It was a unitive view of the individual, religion and the state. Submission to Allah was not limited to one sphere—the private, the personal, the 'religious', the devotional; it was to encompass all of life—the political and legal as well as the personal.

This is why the attempt by some modern commentators to draw a distinction between the inner spiritual *jihad*, by which Muslims struggle to submit personally to Allah, and the outward military *jihad*, whereby the Muslim community struggles to defend itself and expand the borders of Islam by force of arms, ultimately fails. It is an imposition of Western categories, whereby religion is properly private, upon an Islamic worldview in which religion is never private. The personal spiritual *jihad* and the communal political *jihad* are but different aspects or applications of the one idea: that the world, and all the individuals in it, should submit to Allah and his just rule.

Muhammad's programme, then, was to establish a kind of theocracy—a state in which God ruled through his messenger, his prophet, and in which God's law was indistinguishable from the law of the state.

We have not room here (nor do I have the expertise) to trace the working out of this principle over the thousand-year period of Islam's ascendancy in Arabia, Africa, Europe and Asia. In practice, the realities of political power, and the cultural and ethnic diversity of Islamic communities, meant that over the centuries, Islamic states differed considerably in their application of the shariah within the political structures of society. As is the way of things, kings and caliphs tended to have a greater attachment to power and wealth than to the dictates of Allah, and the place of Islam within 'Islamic' states and empires waxed and waned according to political expediency.

Over the past 200 years, and particularly during the last century, the issue of how *shariah* and the traditions of Islam relate to the formation and structures of modern nations has become particularly piquant for many Islamic countries. The increasing dominance of the West industrially, scientifically, technologically and militarily has prompted much Islamic soul-searching. Have we failed to adapt Islam to the demands of the modern world, Muslim intellectuals have asked? Can there be a place for democracy, and for the 'privatising' of Islam, within a more open Western-style society? Are the laws and structures of a seventh century Arabic community adequate any longer to regulate a twenty-first century industrialised nation? And if not, how can they be altered or reformed without gutting the integrity of Islam?

This has been an agonizing question over which much blood has been spilled. As mentioned earlier, many of the key Islamic radical movements (such as the Muslim Brotherhood in Egypt) have arisen not out of a desire to conquer the West but to defend Islam from what they see as erosion from within. The failure of Islamic societies to match the success of the West is due to their apostasy from true Islam, the reformists argue. We do not need to ape the degeneracy of the West, they suggest, but to return to the pure and original word of the Prophet. As Gilles Keppel has suggested, in so arguing, these reform movements managed to mobilise not only the alienated and oppressed urban poor, but the devout Islamic middle-class who viewed the religious laxity of their governments with alarm.

The underlying problem is that the basic structures of Islamic thought, articulated in the Qur'an, the *hadith*, and in centuries of Islamic jurisprudence and tradition, see little place for a 'privatising' of religion. As Allah is one, so society should be one, unified in submission to the pure and godly law which regulates all of life for the good of mankind. This framework stubbornly resists the relativising or marginalizing of religious belief to the private sphere. In a theocracy, God cannot be shut up in private; he must be on the throne, ruling through his representatives, and by his divine law.

Putting the matter in this way makes it clear just how much the Islamic perspective has in common with another ancient religion of the Book: the Judaism of the Old Testament.

The biblical answer

It may seem somewhat odd to skip back at this point from Islam to the Hebrew Bible (or Christian Old Testament), but the reasons for doing so will soon become clear.

Muhammad claimed to be in direct continuity with the revelation of God in the Old and New Testaments, and to merely bring to completion that which those two earlier documents pointed towards. He was the final prophet, the great prophet to end all prophets, bringing in the final and purest version of God's law, which the Old and New

Testaments foreshadowed.

What becomes readily apparent on even a cursory reading of the documents themselves, however, is that Muhammad's conception of the place of God/Allah and his law in society is very much the religion of the Old Testament, rather than the New Testament.

In the history of God's dealings with Israel, recorded in the Old Testament, the promises made to Abraham are fulfilled by the rescue of the Israelites from Egypt, their receipt of the Law on Mt Sinai, their conquest of the promised land, and the establishment of the kingdom of Israel, with David and Solomon as their ideal, golden-age kings. Old Testament Israel is a theocracy, a holy nation with God's law as their statute book, and God's anointed king on the throne.

However, what is quite clear both from the promises leading up to the establishment of national Israel, and from the further prophetic promises that are made after its decline and fall, is that the paradigm of Israel as a theocratic nation-state was only one phase in God's plans. The bigger picture that the Old Testament as a whole presents is of a redemption extending to all humanity, not just one nation—a redemption that blasts through geopolitical boundaries and categories, and establishes the rule of God across racial, ethnic and political boundaries throughout the world.

It is this hope that the New Testament goes on to claim has been fulfilled in Jesus. In defiance of the expectations of many of his contemporaries, Jesus did not see his mission as a politico-military one (to expel the occupying Romans and re-establish the golden age of the Israelite monarchy).

As he so succinctly said to Pilate, "My kingdom is **not of this world**. If my kingdom were of this world, my servants would have been fighting, that I might not be delivered over to the Jews. But my kingdom is not from the world" (John 18:36).

There is a great deal more that could be said about Jesus' claims, and the nature of the 'kingdom' that he claimed to be bringing, but for our purposes here, the point is simple enough. Jesus, and the Christian movement that he started, claimed to fulfil the Old Testament hopes of a revival of God's kingdom—*but not by establishing earthly geopolitical rule*. The kingdom of God that Jesus pointed to was a future heavenly kingdom, a spiritual one, whose influence was felt in the present, but which all the same remained future.

This is the consistent message of the New Testament: that to be a Christian is to give one's complete allegiance to Jesus as God's anointed king (or 'Christ'), and to wait for his coming again, when he will establish once and for all his worldwide kingdom. In the meantime, Christians are to be loyal and obedient members of whatever political arrangements they find themselves in—to "render to Caesar what is Caesar's"—while seeking to spread through their words and actions, the values, attitudes and behaviours of God's eternal kingdom.

The New Testament, in other words, contains a different paradigm of 'church' and 'state' from the Old Testament. It's a paradigm in which God's kingdom and rule is 'hidden' in this present age, and spreads slowly through society by preaching and persuasion, and the formation of communities of faith (or 'churches').

The long history of the West

If the preceding section seems rather theological, it is for good reason. To understand something of how the Western conception of the separation of 'church' and 'state' developed, we must appreciate the basically Christian concepts that formed the boundaries of the discussion.

And a very long discussion it was. The early place of Christianity within the West was one of uneasy co-existence, with frequent outbreaks of fierce persecution (Christians to the lions and all that). But with the conversion to Christianity of the Emperor Constantine in the early 4th century, things took a decisive and fateful turn. For more than a millennia, the nexus between 'church' and 'state' became almost unbreakable. The Roman Catholic Church came to see itself as the very kingdom of God on earth, and its Popes viewed themselves as princes, waging war against all who stood in their way, doctrinally and politically.

But the fact that the primary sources—the New Testament—stood in tension with this developing 'establishment' of Christianity did not escape the notice of Christian thinkers.

Even St Augustine, who sanctioned the use of state force against heretics, saw that there were always two 'cities' in operation—the city of God which was heavenly and eternal, and the earthly city that belonged to this age, and would ultimately come to nothing. As long as this age lasted, the two would be intertwined, and ultimately not discernible; that is, the 'city of God' was still a hidden city, and not to be equated with any earthly institution, political or religious.

However, it was not until the earthquake of the Reformation in the 16th century, and the theological, philosophical and political aftershocks that flowed from it, that the concept of 'Christendom' as a political entity began to break down. Martin Luther asserted with his characteristic vigour that there were two kingdoms, the spiritual and temporal, and that one could not be identified with the other.

Tracing how what we now might call the 'separation of church and state' worked itself out over the ensuing three centuries is a task beyond our scope here. The main point, however, is simple enough. At its core, Christianity is not a theocratic movement. It does not aim to establish the kingdom of God on earth politically. Its view of history and the end of the world is such that it can live and thrive within a range of political arrangements: totalitarian, monarchical, republican. Christianity can exist, with complete integrity, in various kinds of 'states' precisely because establishing a particular kind of polity or state is not one of its aims.

The idea of a 'secular' state, then, which rules and regulates the affairs of 'this age' is quite consistent with the teachings of Jesus and the New Testament (the word 'secular' comes from the Latin meaning 'of this age'). And we are tempted to say that it is no accident that the societies in which this model of church/state relations has flourished have been nations with a Christian (and in particular, a Protestant) heritage.

By contrast, Muhammad, in his adoption of a theocratic conception of God's rule on earth, lays a foundation upon which it is very hard to build a modern democratic nation, with a secular state.

Part 2: Islam and the secular society

We started by posing the question of the place of religious belief in human society. So far, we have addressed only part of that question: that is, how religious belief relates to the state (i.e. government), and the differences between Islam and Christianity in this regard.

However, we must now proceed to the second aspect of the question, and that is this: in a modern nation, with a secular state (or government), *what should be the role and place of religion within society as a whole?*

The answer that most Western societies have gradually come to over the past 200 years has been: 'very little or none at all'. The trend in the West has been not only towards secular states, but also towards secular societies.

It is very important to note that the two are conceptually different, and one does not necessarily entail the other. A secular state (or government) is one in which the state is not allowed to establish any particular religious belief as normative, nor compel its citizens to adopt any religious belief, nor implement a legislative program to institutionalise and promote religious belief. It is a form of political arrangement where the state neither promotes nor persecutes religious belief.

However, a secular state does not have to govern a secular society. In fact, the laws, constitution and traditions of a state will inevitably reflect the religious beliefs of its citizens. Thus, the United States is in some ways the model secular state, with a strict church–state separation built into its constitution. Yet the US still prints 'In God we Trust' on its currency, and has many laws, institutions and structures that are shaped by Christian beliefs and morality. Australia, which likewise has a secular government that neither promotes nor persecutes any religion, still opens its parliamentary proceedings with the Lord's Prayer, has religious education in public schools, and funds Army Chaplains. In other words, a secular state does not imply anything about the actual beliefs of its citizens, who may be religious to a greater or lesser extent, and will bring to their public life together a set of values shaped and formed by their religious convictions, whatever they may be.

However, beginning with the Enlightenment in the late 18th century, and accelerating during the last 100 years or so, there has been a movement to *secularize society* as a whole and not just the state. That is to say, religious belief has not only been disestablished; it has been relegated entirely to the private sphere and excluded from a place in the 'public square'. Indeed, it has become increasingly common in Western societies for the secular state to seek actively to secularize society as a whole; that is, to use its power to exclude religious belief and practice from the public realm (the debate in the US about school prayer is a case in point).

Historically, the change has been massive. There was a time in the West when religion was effectively on the throne (the era of 'Christendom'). There was then a period in which, having abdicated the throne, Christian religious convictions still walked abroad in society, were practised, debated and discussed in public forums, influenced parliamentary debate, and had a large stall in the public square. We have arrived now at a moment in history in which religious conviction (Christian or otherwise) belongs only in the parlour. It is something to be talked about only by consenting adults in the privacy of one's lounge-room. We have moved from having a *state* which does not enforce or legislate on behalf of religious belief, to a *society* in which religious belief has no part in the discussion of public policy and ideas.

This movement was perfectly illustrated in the recent debate over embryonic stem-cell research, in which Australian Senator Amanda Vanstone had this to say about those who opposed the research on religious grounds:

> Your religion is your business and no-one else's. When you make your religion an issue, when you drag it into the political domain, in my view you tarnish it.
>
> It follows that I attach little importance to arguments over dogma. Equally I do not turn to the state to legislate for one religious view over another.[2]

Senator Vanstone went on to declare her view that the embryo is just a clump of cells, not a human, and that it would be stupidity to stop research using embryonic stem cells when the possibility exists that it might lead to advancement in knowledge.

The details of the stem-cell debate are not important here. What is significant is the view of religious belief and its place in society. For Senator Vanstone, religious belief, and any opinions on matters of public policy that might flow from it, must be kept private. It is "your business and no-one else's". Senator Vanstone is saying far more than that the state should not legislate for one religious view over another. She is saying that the state should take no account of the religious views of its citizens *whatsoever* in coming to decisions on matters of public policy. Religion belongs in private, and in no way should enter the public domain. Religious claims, or opinions based on them, are not matters for public, rational discussion, and indeed to attempt to make them so is somehow to "tarnish" them.

Notice that Senator Vanstone's pronouncements as to the status of the embryo—that it is just a clump of cells—are made as if they are obvious fact. Of course, it is not. That the embryo is a clump of cells is a matter of observation and fact; that it is *just* a clump of cells is a philosophical value judgement, for which no evidence is presented. It is a declaration of what the speaker deems to be the truth, based upon the framework of beliefs and ideas with which she sees the world. But it is a value judgement which is valid and belongs in the public domain, whereas a value judgement based on any form of religious belief does not—according to Senator Vanstone.

In other words, our society has become secularized. Only 'non-religious' or anti-religious claims, beliefs and value judgements are allowed to be made in the discussion of public issues, on the assumption that religious beliefs belong in an entirely different category—a category of the private, the non-rational, the non-factual.

This secularization of society has a number of problems, not least of which is that raised by Islam. What if the religion you wish to consign to the private realm has no intention of staying there? What if the system of religious belief is stubbornly public and universalist, and insists that all of life, society and politics be encompassed by its claims?

What if, in the name of furthering its cause, a religion embarks on a very public campaign of terror?

As the bullets pass through our bodies we may meekly protest that religion is being tarnished by entering the public realm, but that would seem to be too little too late. What may already be tarnished, if not ruined altogether, is the view that consigns all religious beliefs, claims and discussion to the private realm.

A bit of intellectual history

To understand how we have come to this point and what we might do about it, we need to understand just a little of the intellectual history of the West. For although the movement towards the secularisation of society as a whole has run in parallel with the separation of church and state, the two are not the same, nor does one lead inevitably to the other. The concept of a secular government—that is, one that is not the church, but which rules over the affairs of society, including the secular affairs of the church itself— is quite compatible with Christian (especially Protestant) belief. A reading of European and American history from 1550-1900 makes that fairly plain.

However, during that time, and especially in the late 18th and 19th centuries, Western thought took a crucial twist. Under the influence of philosophers such as Rousseau and Kant, Western thought tried to construct a view of the world in which humanity could know things truly on the basis of rational thought alone, without defer- ence to some transcendent authority (such as church tradi- tion or 'God'). Rather than starting with God, and building a view of reality upon that, these philosophers started with humanity, and with the world as a closed system of natural causes. Let us not assume God, they argued. Let us start with the world and with man, and think our way out from there, from what we can rationally discover and deduce.

To understand the view that emerged as the dominant one, let us think about reality as a big house, with an upstairs and a downstairs. Upstairs is the world of the divine, of God and faith in him, the realm of love, religion and value. Downstairs is what we could call the 'natural' world, the realm of facts, events, physical causes and mathematics. Prior to the enlightenment, philosophers worked on the assumption that there was a big, broad staircase linking upstairs with downstairs, and that the God who lived upstairs gave meaning, goodness and value to what was downstairs. The two were closely connected, and philosophers and theologians came up with various ways of describing that connection, and the whole. They sought for a theory to make sense of everything, both the upstairs and the downstairs, together, linked and united in one great system of thought.

However, the thinkers of the Enlightenment (and those that followed them) began to doubt whether there really was anything or anyone upstairs, or at least whether there was any such thing as a staircase. Let us stop using the staircase, they suggested, and see if we can work everything out, just using what we can see and think about downstairs.

This presented a thorny problem, because everyone recognized that there *were* such things as beauty and love and value in the world, and indeed that most people recognized the existence of a God. These things were a universal part of human experience. But the solid basis for anchoring and understanding these things was being abandoned. How could we find an agreed common way to talk about these things, if all that we can know is what we have here downstairs?

The idea became entrenched in Western thinking that the universe is a closed system, where there is no access to any supposed 'god' upstairs telling us what to do or think, or establishing absolutes. Facts are solid and can be tested, but values and religious beliefs are elusive and very difficult to agree about. Facts are facts, and can be debated and discussed on rational grounds, and the evidence for them assessed; but religious belief belongs in a different, non-rational realm. Decisions and opinions about religious matters must be decided by the individual, on whatever basis they see fit, but they can't be universalised, because there's no solid, rational basis for doing so, no transcendent authority which can be appealed to in order to establish the rightness or wrongness, the truth or error, of those claims. It's a closed system. The only route to any kind of 'upstairs' (where universal values or God might live) is by exiting the system in some way.

Thus, religious belief and all other claimants to value can only be arrived at by personal conviction, by some non-rational leap of 'faith', a leap upstairs. Religion, in this way of thinking, is a matter of feeling and intuition rather than thought. Faith is an experience of going beyond this world, rather than dealing with this world. If God does exist, he or she is not something that can be discussed or talked about rationally and publicly, because he or she is not really knowable in a rational way. The best one can do is decide, in an act of pure faith, to believe that God exists and has certain characteristics. But this is a personal decision, and cannot be imposed or urged upon others.

Back to Islam

It becomes apparent why Islam presents such a problem for the Western secular worldview. We have consigned religion to the unknowable upstairs, and thus to the realm of the personal, and the unknowable, to those things that are matters of 'faith' but about which we cannot make judgements of 'true' and 'false'. But Islam refuses to stay upstairs, and to remain private and personal. Certain practitioners of Islam come roaring downstairs with a rifle in their hands threatening to shoot us. Radical Islam forces us to a decision, to a value judgement, as to whether we join its cause or oppose it.

But to do so, we have to re-open the staircase. We want to say that Islam is wrong, but we feel we can't, because that would be to admit that you *can* make rational judgements about religion, that one religion might be wrong. And if one is wrong, then another may be wrong as well, and still another may be right. As soon as you admit that it's possible to make rational judgements about religious belief, you're opening up the staircase again, and allowing there to be free trade between the world of facts and evidence and truth, and the world of beliefs and God. You're admitting that, in theory at least, it might be possible to know the truth not just about science and natural events, but about God and faith.

The challenge of Islam exposes the flaw in this way of thinking about religious belief and truth. Where all matters of God and religious belief are consigned to an unknowable and non-rational upstairs, it is impossible to critique religious belief rationally, or to debate its claims. The modern secularist has closed off the possibility of rationally critiquing Islam (or Christianity or any other religion) by removing the whole category of religious belief from normal, rational discussion. And so we are prevented from undertaking the critique that, instinctively, we wish to make.

We want tolerance but have ended up with relativism.

1. S. Abul A'la Mawdudi, *Jihad in Islam,* Pakistan: Islamic Publications, 1998, pp. 3, 15.
2. Quoted in Laura Tingel, "Vanstone: Keep God out of stem cell issue", *Australian Financial Review*, 8/7/02, p 5.

7

MICHAEL LET THE MANUSCRIPT fall into his lap. He glanced over at me with a look that could only be described as quizzical.

"I thought this book was supposed to be about Islam", he said.

I gave a little snort. "So did I."

We were sitting again on the deck, looking out over Michael's backyard. It was Monday afternoon, around 3:30. The afternoon sea breeze had arrived, and was stirring the leaves of the crepe myrtle behind the clothesline. With Dylan at work excavating in his usual corner, and the sun still providing some late autumn warmth, it was hard to believe that the world was not a safe and beautiful place. It seemed a world away—it was a world away— from the mammoth and grizzly excavation work that continued at 'Ground Zero', as the Americans called the World Trade Centre site.

"I'm not saying this is not very interesting", Michael went on. "In fact, it's quite an education. I've never studied much history or any philosophy. And so it was interesting to have a bit of that. Although I found it pretty heavy."

"Yes, that's the worry", I said. "The trouble is, I think the heavy stuff is just necessary. I'm now convinced that we can *understand* Islam all we like; but we won't be in a position to *respond* to it intelligently unless we confront some of these problems. I mean, that's why you got to the point when we talked last time of saying that you wanted to oppose Islam and say that, at least in part, it was 'wrong', but felt you couldn't. It's because of assumptions that I tried to uncover in this chapter."

There was a pause.

"What about we talk about it in two halves", I suggested. "What about the first part on church and state. Did you have any questions or comments on that part?"

"Not really. I mean, it flowed on pretty logically from the previous chapters. You'd already talked about how Islam doesn't really have a church/state distinction. But I hadn't really thought about why we *do* have that distinction in our society. How it relates to Christianity, I mean."

He flipped through the pages. "So are you saying that the Old Testament was more your Islamic-style, totalitarian God, whereas the New Testament God was more in favour of democracy?"

I laughed. "Well people have often tried to drive a wedge between the two testaments, but I'm not sure they've ever tried it on the basis of which one was the more democratic! The thing is, the Christian Bible is built round a story, a narrative. It goes somewhere. There's progression, and change. What God is trying to do unfolds over centuries. So there are different phases in the plan, but I guess I'd like to say that it was the same God behind it all."

"Yeah I guess you would…"

It has always been my experience that when the word 'God' pops up in a conversation, things very quickly either get fairly animated and heated, or else very quiet and awkward. This one seemed to be heading in the latter direction, and so I was a little surprised by what Michael said next.

"So how can be you so sure that your God is right and the Muslim God is not?"

I looked back at him to see if he was joking, but he was returning my look intently.

"Do you think that's what I'm saying in the chapters so far?" I asked.

"Not in so many words, but the implication's there. Christianity leads to open, democratic societies; Islam doesn't. That seems to be your line."

"It's not quite as simple as that. It is fair to say that the categories of Christian thought have given rise to a separation of church and state, and to a climate in which modern democracy could grow. It's also true, though, that there have been times when Christianity was in its earlier 'Christendom' phase, when it yielded anything but an open, free society. But I don't think that Islam carries the same flexibility and potential—that's my own view."

Michael was becoming animated. "But is that enough to say—outright—that Islam is 'wrong'?"

"Not at all", I replied. "We can't even begin to discuss whether Islam is 'true' or 'wrong' until we're prepared to admit that it is possible—in theory—for a religious belief or claim to be 'true' or 'wrong'. And a great many people in our society simply won't do that."

"That's your upstairs, downstairs thing."

"Yes", I said. "Did that make sense?"

"Sort of. I certainly think it's fair enough to say that religion and God are mostly left out of the discussion these days. It's seen as a matter for each person individually. I suppose I'm surprised that you want it to be any other way."

"What do you mean?"

"Well you want us to open up religion and belief—all that stuff—for public debate. You seem to want us to get to a point where we can say something like 'Islam is basically wrong' (for example) or Buddhism or whatever. But you're a Christian. Aren't you worried that we all might decide that Christianity is basically wrong? Doesn't that possibility bother you?"

"Well, in one sense I guess it does, but it mainly excites me."

Michael shook his head. "I don't get it."

"It excites me because if Christianity could possibly be wrong (and Islam and Buddhism and the rest), then it could also possibly be right. If you admit that a certain claim is a truth claim, and can be possibly falsified, then it can also possibly be established as true and reasonable.

"And that gives me hope, because I think that's basically how we need to respond to Islam as a society. I don't think we should ban it, or censor it, or oppress Muslims, or keep them out. What we need to do is *critique* Islam, to argue with it, to hold its claims up to scrutiny, to discuss together in the public square whether such-and-such is a valid claim, whether it is reasonable, whether ultimately it is true. This is the very point at which we've stumbled a couple of times as we've talked. We've started to say that we think Islam is wrong at some point, or made some value judgement about it, and then looked at one another with a guilty look as if we've just committed a terrible sin. But it's not a sin. The terrible sin, I think, is to *fail to critique* Islam and Christianity and Atheism."

Michael looked at me intently, and then shook his head again. "I hear what you're saying. But I don't see how it would be possible. How can you test or prove or falsify a religion? Such as Islam or such as Christianity? Aren't they dealing with things that are not open to proof? Isn't that what religion is, almost by definition? I guess that's the problem I have."

Michael looked out into the backyard. "I have another problem too".

"What's that?" I asked.

"Dylan's gone" said Michael, and bounded down into the backyard to search for Dylan who, it turned out, had crawled down behind the shed and out the back gate, and was on his way down the rear lane towards the main road.

I went back for my papers and notes, and stopped to say goodbye to Michael who had a squirming Dylan under his arm.

"Listen, that was really good. I don't know where exactly it leads, but I'll try to do something next on your last question, which was how on earth you would prove or falsify a religion, like Islam."

"Sure", said Michael. "But like I said before, I'm still interested in what Islam teaches about women. Don't forget that."

I grimaced and muttered something about seeing what I could do, and headed for home.

8

I SAT AGAIN AT MY desk surrounded by a mound of photo-copied articles, books and magazines, not sure where to go next.

Logically, the next step in the book was to address the question of truth with respect to religion. Is it possible to have 'truth' and 'religious belief' in the same sentence? Do they belong in the same category? And so can we talk about Islam (or Buddhism or Christianity) in those terms? In terms of our conversation, it was the next topic, but as to where the book was going, I was becoming increasingly uncertain.

In any case, for Michael, the more pressing issue seemed to be the status of women within Islam, and I was beginning to guess why. I felt I should at least attempt to put something together on the topic, although the prospect hardly filled me with joy.

This was for two reasons. To start with, sorting out what 'Islam' taught about women was even more difficult than wading through the claims and counter-claims about violence and jihad. Since the rise of feminism, Islamic apologists have repeatedly claimed that Islam is unique amongst world religions in treating women with enormous dignity, respect and equality. A picture has been painted of Islamic culture as a haven for women, in which they were granted rights (such as being able to own property) more than a millennium before this took place in the Christianised West.

Again, however, the picture is by no means that simple. These apologists routinely ignore or omit those parts of the Qur'an and hadith that prejudice their case—such as parts in which wife-beating is condoned, or in which woman is characterised as man's intellectual and spiritual inferior, and so on.

The second complicating factor is that, as Westerners, we hardly approach the whole question of the status of women from a position of strength, let alone neutrality. We may decry the conditions under which women live in many Islamic countries, and regard the treatment of women as oppressive and primitive. Yet from the Islamic side, we hardly have a lot to boast about. 'What has your 20th century social revolution brought you?' they might ask. And if we were to reply honestly we would have to say that although some injustices have been righted, and some freedoms established, we have also seen a calamitous rise in divorce and relational breakdown, teenage pregnancy, single-motherhood, sexually transmitted disease, pornography and its exploitation of women and children, and the list goes on. We would hardly say that the position of women in Western society is one of unremitting joy and happiness.

All of which meant that I wanted to leave the subject of 'women in Islam' alone. It just seemed like too much of a can of worms. I had a deep suspicion that the Islamic publicity campaign about how wonderful Islam was for women was just that: a publicity campaign. The reality, as far as I could tell, was that women were not treated well in most Islamic cultures around the world. Certainly, my own anecdotal knowledge of Western women who had married Muslim men was not encouraging. During the courtship it was all 'Islam treats women with dignity and true freedom'; after the marriage, a different picture emerged, in which the husband expected the wife to obey him completely and be his servant, sexually and in all other respects.

But how could this be proved or even argued?

What's more, I didn't think this was where the logic of the book was taking me. It was getting to be about the slippery subject of 'truth', and whether it was legitimate or not to say that Islam was 'wrong'. This is what I wanted to explore next.

I decided to put something together on this topic, and chat further to Michael about the 'women in Islam' thing later on.

Michael,

Here's the next bit. It's about that issue of 'truth' we talked about. Warning: the following text contains scenes of graphic argument about truth and falsehood, which some readers may find offensive!

(As for 'women', I'll chat to you about that next Monday.)

T.

So far, our goal has been to understand Islam, in its essence and in all its diversity, and to assess the extent to which Islam itself is integral to the current world conflicts.

However, as we have done so, it has become clear that we will not have done our subject justice until we go one step further. We must try to assess not only the truth *about* Islam, but the truth *of* Islam, for one of the key facets of Islam is its claim to truth. Muhammad did not emerge from the cave with an opinion as to how society might arrange itself; he came with what he claimed was a revelation from God himself, utterly true and universally applicable for all mankind. Islam claims to be *the* truth, the ultimate word from the God who made the world as to what is true and how we should live.

A very common recent response to the truth claims of Islam (and any other religion) has been 'relativism'—the view that something is only 'true' relative to the individual or group who holds it be true. The relativist will happily allow Muslims to claim universal truth, Christians also to claim universal truth, and at the same time atheists to say that they are both wrong. For the relativist, everything is a form of opinion. There is no such thing as a 'truth' about which we might argue; we must all simply allow each other to claim mutually contradictory things as being true, and then get on with life as if it didn't matter.

The logical impossibility of that position is clear from a moment's reflection. However, the *practical* impossibility of relativism was made equally clear on September 11. Claims to truth—religious or otherwise—cannot be separated from their political, historical and social consequences in the world. It may be possible, for a short time, to pretend that all claims to 'truth' and 'right' are equally valid and that it doesn't really matter; but when, on the basis of my 'truth' I do something which is profoundly offensive to you (such as kill thousands of people), all of a sudden it does matter. It matters a great deal.

The question, then, of whether Islam—as a system of religious belief—is *true* is a vital one. It is especially important if we are to maintain the hard-won Western tradition of a tolerant and open society. Because *tolerance* is very different from *relativism*.

As it has been historically expressed, tolerance is the willingness to live side by side with people with whom you disagree, as expressed in the famous saying, "I disapprove of what you say, but I will defend to the death your right to say it". Relativism, on the other hand, is the removal of the possibility of either agreeing or disagreeing, since there is no 'truth' to agree about. There is just a multitude of personally held views, each of which is as valid as the other.

A tolerant society values discussion, disagreement and persuasion, and allows freely for the possibility of changing one's position, since the truth is something we can argue about. Relativist societies often cease to be tolerant, because they outlaw disagreement. In a relativist society, the statement "You are wrong" is not allowed. Since rational argument and debate about truth-claims are put to one side, all that is left is prejudice, cultural preference, tribal/family allegiance and political power. The phenomenon of 'political correctness', although now often joked about, is a manifestation of the intolerance of relativist societies. There are certain thoughts, ideas or philosophies that are not allowed to be expressed in some contexts, because they are utterly offensive to the ruling group in that context. To express them, in whatever form, is to risk censure, ridicule, harassment or worse. It would be a brave lecturer, for example, who sought to mount a critique of feminist thought in a university humanities department. It's not that he/she would be bound to lose the argument; they would be bound to lose their job.

The irony of this situation is one of the features of modern Western society—that those who most vehemently deny the concept of absolute truth are the ones who most vehemently suppress open debate and the expression of alternative viewpoints.

How do we accept something as 'true'

It must be said, however, that Western society is currently only partly relativistic. Truth and error, right and wrong—these are still categories that most people accept and act upon in their daily lives. When someone tells us a lie, and we find out that it was a lie, not many of us say, "Well, perhaps that was true for you, but it wasn't true for me". We are more likely to say, "Why did you lie to me? What you told me wasn't the truth!"

One area in which Western societies *are* increasingly relativistic (as opposed to tolerant) is religion. Many people think that matters of religion, values and ethics belong in an entirely different category to the rest of life. We may still believe in mathematical and scientific 'truth'—that it is possible to make true statements of fact about the world—but religion, ethics and matters of 'belief' belong in an entirely different realm. They belong 'upstairs' (in the terms used earlier). They are purely matters of opinion and 'faith', and the question of whether they are 'true' cannot be discussed.

This categorisation of faith and religion in one box, and facts and truth in another, has a long history which we have already touched upon. It is a distinction, however, that ultimately doesn't hold up, because the claims of religion and ethical systems cannot be partitioned off from the real world. They exist in the world. They make claims, and assert certain things to be true about the world—and indeed, about the God (or gods) who made the world, and may have some present influence over the world. These claims are either valid or not; that is, they are true or they are not. Either there really is an all-just, all-merciful Allah, who rules all events in this world, or there is not. We may disagree and argue about whether it is true, but it is either true or not. It's nonsensical to say that Allah is God of all the world in one breath, and then to allow that he is not in the next.

On what basis, then, can we assess whether a religious system, or any system of thought, is true? There are endless philosophical debates about questions such as this, but put simply, there are two basic tests that we can apply.

Firstly, we can assess whether a system of belief or philosophy is *internally consistent*; that is, we can check to see if there are contradictions or internal conflicts bound up within the system itself that render it unlikely to be true.

For example, in the system of beliefs and claims called 'astrology', it is claimed that the planets influence events and persons on the earth, depending on their position relative to each other and the stars. In particular, the position and arrangement of the planets at the time of your birth determines the kind of person you are.

There are various questions of internal consistency and coherence that might be asked of astrology, and which cast doubt on the truth of its claims. Chief among them is the fact that the planets and stars are no longer in the positions upon which astrological charts are based. Because of a phenomenon known as the 'procession of the equinoxes', whereby the earth's axis very slowly describes a circle (over 25,800 years), the position of the signs of the zodiac changes in relation to the earth. And so if you were born on January 27th, you are supposedly born under the sign of Aquarius, with all the Aquarian influences shaping your personality. But, according to the actual position of the planets, you are really being born under the sign of Capricorn. This presents a real problem of internal consistency. If the *position* of the planets is what, in some mysterious way, influences a person's nature and personality, and yet the planets have moved in relation to the earth such that they are no longer in that position, then how can they have that particular influence?

Astrologers have no answer to this conundrum, except to say that they are unsure how it all works, but that they are sure that it *does work*.

This brings us to the second test. The most basic way in which humans have always established or tested the truth of a claim is to compare it (and its consequences) with the world outside the system—that is, to 'check it against the world and see'. To the extent that a religion or system of thought makes claims about the world, and events in the world, we can try to see if these claims are ***externally verifiable***, if they can be attested by other sources, and if they give a good account of human experience.

For example, to return to astrology, is it possible to verify the claims of astrological prediction in a real world test? It is not only possible, but has been done on numerous occasions by a range of scientists working in fields such as physics and psychology. Tests and trials have been conducted in which astrological predictions are tested against the personalities of different groups, to see if there is any correlation between what astrology says should be the case (how a personality is influenced by the planets) and whether that effect actually takes place. In test after test, the astrological claims have been shown to be without value.

This presents a real problem for astrology. Based on both the problems of internal coherence, and the evidence of external verification (which goes heavily against it), it would seem very unlikely that the claims of astrology are valid and true. On the available evidence, which is considerable, astrology is not a system of belief worthy of trust, upon which one might base decisions about life.

Let us think then about Islam, and apply these two tests to it.

Internal consistency

As we have noted earlier, Islamic scholars and interpreters do not attempt to deny that there are conflicts or contradictions within the Qur'an and the *hadith*. The common response to these conflicts is the 'principle of abrogation', or *naskh*, whereby later Qur'anic verses supersede earlier ones. This is said to be based on a verse in the Qur'an itself:

> If we abrogate a verse (or message) or cause it to be forgotten, We will replace it by a better one or one similar (Qur'an 2:106).

Some may object that this is a very convenient way to solve problems of internal consistency, especially since it is by no means clear from the Qur'an itself which *suras* are earlier or later, and thus which verse should abrogate which. There is no narrative development or storyline within the Qur'an to indicate how, for example, a changed circumstance might require a different form of action. That information can only be inferred from the *hadiths*, the collection of the Prophet's deeds and sayings, which is used to try to locate the various *suras* in his career, and thus determine which ones should be abrogated.

The most pressing difficulty, however, is not working out which teaching should cancel out the other, but explaining why such contradictory teachings should exist in the first place. This is particularly so given the exalted claims that are made on behalf of the Qur'an regarding its divine origin and perfection. According to the book itself, the Qur'an comes direct from Allah (55:1-2), a transcript of an eternal, heavenly book in Allah's keeping (43:1-2), which is sent down upon the Prophet Muhammad without error or contradiction (4:82; 18:1; 55:1-2), and is preserved from all corruption by Allah himself (56:77-80). The idea that such a revelation should contain contradictory statements and instructions is hard to reconcile.

However, apart from these problems with individual statements or prohibitions in the Qur'an, there is a deeper logical problem that confronts Islam, although it is not often recognized or discussed: the problem of justice and mercy.

The Qur'an (and subsequent Islamic teaching) holds that Allah is all-wise, all-seeing and all-just. He is the just judge of all the earth, and will bring every act to judgement at the Last Day. On the Judgement Day, when the trumpet sounds, every person will receive his due, according to what he has done:

> The earth shall beam with the light of its Lord, and the Book shall be laid down, and the prophets and the witnesses shall be brought up, and judgement shall be given between them with justice, and they shall not be dealt with unjustly.
>
> And every soul shall be paid back fully what it has done, and He knows best what they do.
>
> And those who disbelieve shall be driven to hell in companies...
>
> And those who are careful of their duty to their Lord shall be conveyed to the garden (paradise) in companies...
>
> And you shall see the angels going round the

throne glorifying the praise of their Lord; and judgement shall be given between them with justice, and
it shall be said: All praise is due to Allah, the Lord of
the worlds.

(Qur'an 39:69-75; also see 7:7)

The purity and justice of Allah is beyond questioning, and
because of his omniscience even an atom of goodness will
not go unrewarded, or an atom of evil unpunished.

However, Muhammad also teaches, in countless places
throughout the Qur'an, that Allah is all-merciful. Every
sura (except one) in the Qur'an is introduced by the
bismallah formula: "In the Name of Allah, the Beneficent,
the Merciful". Allah is frequently praised in the Qur'an as
the fount of all graciousness, compassion, mercy and
forgiveness.

The logical or ethical problem here is simple: upon
what basis can Allah be both all-just and all-merciful?
Justice would demand that all sins be punished, and that
no wrong-doing be passed over. Yet the very concept of
'forgiveness' or 'mercy' is that sins *are* passed over or left
unpunished. How is it fair or just that one guilty person
be rightly punished for their sin, and another forgiven for
that same sin? Justice would demand that wrongdoing
should always receive its due recompense.

This is a problem shared of course by Christianity. How
is that God can forgive imperfect, sinful humans without
compromising his own standards of perfect justice?
(Christianity proposes an answer to the dilemma, which we
may come back to in due course.)

The answer of Islamic teaching to all these sorts of
dilemmas (whether of commands being abrogated or

seeming inconsistencies in Allah's actions) is to take refuge in the inscrutable and ultimately unknowable will of Allah. Allah is all-supreme and all-powerful. He can do as he wishes, and he is not bound by earthly standards of consistency. If he condemns an action at one point, his will is not bound by that decision. He is free to decree otherwise at any future point, such is his complete and unbounded sovereignty. If he wishes to forgive, he will; if he wishes to punish, he will. If there seems to be an inconsistency in this, the answer lies beyond the veil. It is locked up in the unknowable and unapproachable person of Allah.

This is a dissatisfying and ultimately inadequate answer. It is perfectly legitimate to say that our knowledge of Allah and his will is not complete or comprehensive; one does not have to know everything about a person to still know him truly. But when that person does reveal himself, and does so in a way that is claimed to be complete, non-contradictory and perfect, then it is reasonable to require that the revelation make sense within itself. The clash of Allah's justice and mercy present a logical and ethical difficulty for the Islamic system of belief that has never been satisfactorily answered.

Let us turn from these difficulties to the second of our tests—the external test.

External tests

The Qur'an, unlike the Christian Bible, is not a book much concerned with history. It does not relate many historical figures or happenings, or describe many real-world events. Most of its sayings are more timeless and universal, describing Allah, and the way people should live in submission to him.

However, there are points at which we can 'test' the truth of the Islamic belief system against the world in which we live. One very simple but important test concerns the death of Jesus of Nazareth.

Jesus is an important and venerated figure in Islam, and is of course central to Christianity. However, the two state quite different things about his death. In the Qur'an, Muhammad asserts quite forcefully that Jesus *was not* crucified and *did not* die:

> They said, "We killed Christ Jesus the son of Mary, the Apostle of God," but they killed him not, nor crucified him, but so it was made to appear to them, and those who differ therein are full of doubts with no certain knowledge, but only conjecture to follow. For a surety they killed him not; Nay, God raised him up unto Himself, and God is Exalted in Power, Wise (Qur'an 4:157-8).

The Christian Bible, of course, repeatedly affirms the exact opposite, that Jesus *was* crucified and *did* die. This quote from Paul's letter to the Corinthians is just one of many instances in the New Testament:

> Now I would remind you, brothers, of the gospel I preached to you, which you received, in which you stand, and by which you are being saved, if you hold fast the word I preached to you—unless you believed in vain.
>
> For I delivered to you as of first importance what I also received: that Christ died for our sins in accor-

dance with the Scriptures, that he was buried, that he was raised on the third day in accordance with the Scriptures... (1 Corinthians 15:1-4).

There is little room for ambiguity or misunderstanding in these passages. This is not an obscure difference of interpretation about some fine point of theology. Claiming to speak the true and inspired words of God, Muhammad states quite clearly that, as a matter of history, Jesus was not crucified. By contrast, the most basic historical claim of Christianity is that Jesus was in fact crucified, that he died and was buried.

This presents us with an unavoidable choice. If Islam is true at this point, then Christianity is profoundly false. For if the Qur'an is right in saying that Jesus did not really die, then the great edifice of Christian belief collapses like a house of cards. Without the death of Jesus, Christianity is next to meaningless.

However, the converse also holds. If Jesus did in fact die, then Islam is false—for Islam claims that the Qur'an is the pure and unadulterated word of God, perfect and true in every respect. If the Qur'an is shown at this point to be flat wrong, then one of the central claims of Islam also comes tumbling down.

There is, of course, a third possibility—that is, that both are wrong. It could be that Jesus never lived. The truth of the matter must lie in one of these three directions, not as a matter of cultural preference or personal background or family custom. Logically, it can be expressed in the form of a diagram:

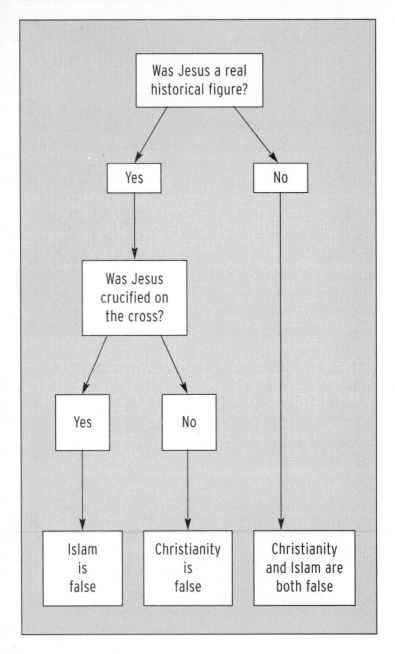

We will return to the implications of this choice below, but for now we need to establish the truth, one way or the other. As a matter of history, was Jesus a real historical figure, and was he crucified or not?

On the question of whether Jesus actually lived or not, we need not dwell too long. No serious historian, Jewish, Christian or atheist, doubts it. The documentary evidence is overwhelming, from both 'Christian' sources (such as the New Testament itself), and non-Christian sources (such as Josephus and Tacitus, which we will touch on below in relation to his death). That Jesus of Nazareth did live and exist, being born some time around 4 BC, is not seriously in dispute. That leaves us with the other two options that revolve around the fact (or otherwise) of his death. Where are we to look for the answer to that question?

There is the witness, first of all, of the 27 books of the New Testament itself. The nature of his death, and the circumstances under which it took place, are described in detail in the four Gospels, and there are countless further references to it in the letters and other documents that make up the rest of the New Testament. On almost every page, the death of Jesus on the cross is either explicitly affirmed, or else assumed, argued from or incidentally referred to. To excise the death of Jesus on the cross from the New Testament would be to leave very little.

What is more, the vast majority of scholars agree that all four Gospels were written by the end of the first century at the latest. That is, these documents, based on eye-witness testimony, were written within a generation or two of the events they describe. They were written within the life-times of people who could contradict the version of events they portrayed. It is inconceivable that the Gospel accounts could have survived as they have if their portrayal of the central event of the story—that is, the death of Jesus—was a fabrication.

It is also inherently unlikely that such a story *would* be fabricated. Execution on a cross was no romantic ideal for first century revolutionaries. It was an utterly barbarous form of death, designed by the Romans to be as painful and as humiliating as possible. It is hardly the kind of end that a Jewish Messianic movement would invent for its hero.

The evidence of the New Testament itself would seem to suggest, very strongly, that Jesus was in fact crucified.

However, there is also evidence from non-Christian historians of the period that serves to confirm the New Testament version of events. Josephus, the first century Jewish historian, writes about Jesus that Pilate "condemned him to be crucified".[1] Tacitus, an eminent Roman historian of the period, says much the same:

> Christus, from whom the name [Christians] had its origin, suffered the extreme penalty during the reign of Tiberius at the hands of one of our procurators, Pontius Pilatus, [in] Judaea.[2]

It is hardly surprising, then, that the overwhelming consensus of scholarly opinion, whether Christian or non-Christian (though not Islamic), is that Jesus of Nazareth was in fact crucified at the order of Pontius Pilate some time around 30 AD.

Against this evidence, Muhammad, writing some 600 years after the events, claims to have received a divine revelation which emphatically denies that Jesus was crucified. It must be noted that Muhammad's claim was not on the basis of some ancient copy of the New Testament that he had gotten his hands on that told a different story. He did not argue in this fashion. He simply asserted the non-crucifixion as a matter of divine revelation.

In an effort to support the Qur'an's teaching that Jesus was not crucified, Muslim apologists claim that the New Testament we have is a corrupted version, and that there once existed a pure 'original' Gospel that agreed with the Qur'an's insistence that Jesus did not die. Some Muslim scholars even cite 'The Gospel of Barnabas' as a version of this original uncorrupted text.

This can only be described as an argument of desperation. Thousands of very early copies and fragments of the New Testament survive from the first five centuries AD, none of which differ from one another in any but the most minor of copying errors. The New Testament of our time is the same as the New Testament of the first century—and indeed the same as the New Testament of Muhammad's time. There is ample manuscript evidence to demonstrate this. There is simply no credible evidence whatsoever of an alternative 'uncorrupted' New Testament that tells a different story (that Jesus was not crucified). As for 'The Gospel of Barnabas', no reputable New Testament scholar (Jew, Christian or atheist) gives it any credence. It shows every mark of being a medieval forgery, dating from around the 14th century.

By any reasonable test, then, the claim of the Qur'an that Jesus was not in fact crucified, is false. It has no evidence in its favour, and a mountain of evidence against it. It is rather like those lunatic-fringe historians who seek to edit the Holocaust out of World War II. There is just too much evidence, too many people who saw it, and whose testimonies are recorded.

This presents real problems for the integrity of Islamic belief. The Qur'an claims for itself a status of absolute perfection, of being the pure and divine word of Allah, given to Muhammad, and flawlessly written and preserved to this day. It is deemed to be absolutely without error or discrepancy.

Yet at this point of intersection with world events and history, it is found to be in error—unless some startling new evidence might be found that changes that judgement. And given the nature of the case against it, and the weight of evidence, such a reversal seems improbable.

To make such a statement—that Islam, on the basis of the available evidence, is wrong—is of course deemed by many to be the height of rudeness and arrogance. On the contrary, it is really the only honourable and polite thing to do. It is a statement which meets and addresses Islam on its own terms, which takes seriously its claims to be a revelation of ultimate truth.

When the Western secularist dismisses all claims to truth, and declares all religions to be much the same, he insults both the Christian and the Muslim. Perhaps without realising it, he adopts the ultimate high-ground of moral and intellectual superiority, as he addresses both the Muslim and the Christian: "You may each think—in your quaint way—that there is such a thing as truth, and that God has revealed it to you. I, however, can see, from my vantage point quite above such primitive notions, that there is no such thing as truth, and that you in fact really believe the same sorts of things, even though you yourselves assert that you don't. I alone have come to know the truth that there is no religious truth—except mine."

The position of the Western secularist—in declaring that it is impossible ever to assert that one religion might be wrong and another right—is the most patronizing and arrogant stance imaginable.

It is also illogical and unsustainable. September 11 made that clear.

1   Josephus, *Antiquities of the Jews* xviii.63.
2   Tacitus, *Annals of Imperial Rome* xv.44.

9

IT WAS A MISERABLE, rainy afternoon, and the weather had driven us indoors into the family room. Dylan was playing in the corner with his Duplo™. Connor and Kelly weren't yet home from school.

We sat in the lounge-chairs, sipping coffee and trying to get somewhere. Michael was subdued. He sat with his big shoulders slightly rounded, both his hands cupped around the coffee mug, staring into it as if trying to find some words there.

"What about the content of the arguments themselves?" I ventured. "How did they strike you?"

"I don't know, mate", Michael said. "Maybe I'm just not used to thinking like this, but I'm finding it hard to make an intelligent comment. Your basic point was clear enough: that if two things are contradictory, they can't both be right."

"Yes, that was it."

"And so, as to whether Jesus was crucified or not, you've got a fairly clear point of contradiction. Which seems fair. But are they the only options. I mean, even if we accept that Jesus was crucified (which seems pretty likely, I agree) that doesn't mean we have to believe that he is 'God'", said Michael, writing the quote marks in the air.

"Of course not", I replied. "That's not what I was arguing. Whether Jesus was God, and whether the Christian claims in general stand up to scrutiny—well, that's a completely separate question. What I was simply trying to show was that it is possible to make a rational judgement about a set of religious claims, based on internal coherence and external evidence. And that on both those grounds, Islam takes a hammering. The 'crucifixion test' is an interesting one because it forces the two great religions into a fairly clear-cut opposition. They cannot both be right on this basic point of history, and Islam comes off second-best on the available evidence. But that's not to say that therefore Christianity is 'true' in totality. It seems to be true in its claims at this point—that Jesus was crucified—but there's a lot more work to be done before we could say that it is true in *all* its essential claims—such as that Jesus was God in the flesh."

Michael ran his hand through his hair. "I don't know. You make out that it's a choice between truth and error, or right and wrong, but surely it's a matter of faith."

"Depends what you mean by faith."

Michael looked somewhat startled. "Well don't ask me what faith means. You're the religious one!"

"No, I am asking you what *you* mean by 'faith'. When you use the word, what are you thinking when you use it?"

"Oh, I don't know. Something like 'believing in something where there isn't scientific proof'. I mean, you can't prove God can you?"

This reminded me of that line in *The Hitchhiker's Guide to the Galaxy* where God, in a moment of carelessness, does something utterly extraordinary (creating the babel fish) which so obviously proves his existence that it removes the need for 'faith', and God suddenly disappears in a puff of logic.

"The idea of 'faith' as a leap into the dark in the absence of any evidence or facts is *not at all* how the Bible uses the word. The 'leap in the dark' definition is, in fact, precisely a product of the modern idea that subjects like God and religion belong in the unknowable 'upstairs' category—the category of irrationality, of unreality, of other-worldly spooky stuff that can never be the subject of evidence or facts or history. And so, President Bush talks about 'people of faith', and 'faith-based initiatives', as if there is this class of people with this particular characteristic: they believe in spooky other-worldly stuff that has no evidence for it. But that's not what faith is at all."

"So what do you think 'faith' is?"

"It's very simple. It's trusting the truth of something or someone based on the evidence available. You have 'faith' that your wife loves you. That's not a leap in the dark. You have good reason to believe it, because of the evidence—how she treats you, what she says to you, the fact that she is still here, and so on. That's 'faith'. I guess you could replace it with the word 'trust'; it's 'relying on something to be true'. That's why most Westerners don't remotely understand why the terrorists would sacrifice their lives for their cause. They see it as being about 'faith'—this airy mystical quality that some people have—which is all very well, but why would you kill yourself and thousands of people because of 'faith'. But for the terrorists, it wasn't like that at all. They passionately believed Islam to be *true*, and that the US was the Great Satan, their enemy. For that cause, they gladly died."

Michael went quiet. I wasn't sure whether it was because I'd said too much, or whether the whole conversation was becoming alarmingly 'religious' in nature. But I guess that was my point. Putting 'religion' into a separate category—one that was unknowable, personal, irrational and therefore not to be discussed in public—was precisely the problem. Things are true or they're not. Sometimes it's hard to tell whether they are or not—that is, it's hard to get enough evidence to tell one way or the other—but at least you can try, and in principle get there. Why should, say, something like whether Jesus was ever crucified, be any different? Or for that matter the claims he made for himself—about being God's Son for example? Why can't we discuss and debate these questions, and look at the evidence?

Michael continued to say nothing, except a non-committal, "Yeah, well…" which trailed off into the cool afternoon air. I thought that his mind had headed off somewhere else. But then he said, "So what does all this mean for Islam in Australia? It's all very well for us to sit here and talk in theory about religious truth, and evidence, but how does that help me get on with Muslims? I can't see how telling people that their religion is basically wrong is going to do much for the relationship."

"As a matter of fact, I think it's the only way we can peacefully co-exist in the long-term."

"Sorry?"

"Well what are the alternatives? We can ban Islam in Australia, like Menzies tried to ban the Communist Party, but I can't see how that's the way forward. What are you going to do? Deport all the Muslims? Or ban them from Friday prayer? Or sew a special patch on their clothes?"

I was getting a bit warmed up, but Michael didn't seem to mind. I pressed on. "And so, of course, we welcome Muslims into our country, and extend to them the normal freedoms of association and religion that we all enjoy. But as we do so, we currently seem to extend to them all kinds of freedoms except one: the freedom to be wrong. The one thing you're not allowed to do in our current multicultural context is to critique a religious system of beliefs, especially an 'ethnic' one like Islam."

"I remember you saying this before sometime", said Michael.

"Sorry to repeat myself, but I just think it's essential. It's the very thing we must do if we want Muslims to be full and long-term participants in our society. We must be allowed to refute Islam, just as Muslims must be allowed to refute atheism and agnosticism and Christianity—on the kinds of grounds that we've been talking about. We should scrutinise claims, and look at internal coherence and external evidence. We must allow people to think and reason and debate, about all manner of things, including religious beliefs, and to change their position. In other words, *we must love and respect other persons enough to argue with them about the truth.*"

I paused for breath. "The trouble is, it's not happening. In fact the reverse is happening. There is legislation on the books in Victoria, and slated for South Australia, that basically makes it *illegal* to criticise someone's religion."

"You're kidding", said Michael.

"No, not at all. I know of two men who ran a seminar in Melbourne about Islam, and critiqued Islam from a Christian perspective, who are now facing a complaint before the relevant tribunal under the 'Racial and Religious Tolerance Act'."

"Oh please."

"No, I'm serious. When people are not allowed to discuss the truth or otherwise of religious claims, we end up with the suppression of debate and dissent. Certain opinions and views become the 'authorised' ones that are allowed to be expressed, and this is all determined by whoever happens to be in charge. Truth and freedom are gone. All you're left with is the raw exercise of power."

Michael looked at me intently, and then folded his arms and stared out across the backyard. There was a silence, and it seemed like that line of discussion was at an end, at least for the moment.

I was tempted to call it a day, but I decided to take a punt and test out a theory.

"It's Kelly, isn't it?" I asked.

Michael looked at me sharply. "What do you mean 'it's Kelly'?"

"That's why the interest in women and Islam. Kelly's gotten herself mixed up with a Muslim guy."

Michael's eyes narrowed a little, and his face briefly flirted with an I'm-not-giving-anything-away look. He looked down, put his hand up to his forehead, and massaged it between his thumb and fore-finger as if trying to squeeze something out.

He didn't look at me as he spoke. "It's just the latest in a long line of disasters. I don't know what it is with 16-year-old girls. One minute they're your gorgeous little girl whose turning into a lady, and then—bang!—their brain explodes. They hate you, they ignore you, and they go out and try to do as much damage as they can to themselves. It's just unbelievable."

"When did this latest thing start?" I asked.

"It's been going on for a couple of months now. She met this guy down at the club. They're both under-age, but that doesn't seem to stop them getting in. I guess they could both pass as 18."

"Well, he couldn't be all that devout a Muslim if he's down at the club."

"I don't know what sort of Muslim he is. I just know I don't like him, I don't trust him, and I don't want him around my daughter."

There was a pause. At least I was glad I hadn't written a 5000-word dissertation on the teaching of Islam on women. I don't think it would have helped.

"What does Kelly say?"

"She says I'm racist and a bigot, among other things."

"So, are you?"

"Well, I didn't use to think so! I don't really know this kid; he just scares me, that's all. He comes from a big family; they're Lebanese, although he was born here. I have these visions of him treating her like a plaything, and then casting her off when he's finished."

"So you think Muslim boys are the only ones who treat girls like that?"

"Yeah, I know what you're saying. The truth is, I don't even really know this kid. Like I said, I just don't like him or trust him." Michael looked down, and snorted. "I sound like the dad of every girl I ever went out with."

He looked back at me again.

"But what *does* Islam teach about women?"

I sighed. There was nothing for it but to try to give some account of it. I started to explain to Michael the problems; how it was hard to nail down exactly because there was so much propaganda and spin involved; how we had to bear in mind the very different cultural context in which this teaching arose and is practised; and yet how there were aspects of it that remained disturbing. I rambled on for what seemed like an eternity. But then something else occurred to me.

"Michael, even if I was able to sort out for you exactly what Islam taught about women, and summarize it for you, what difference would it make?"

"To me, you mean?"

"To Kelly."

There was a silence.

"The simple fact is", I went on, "that whatever Islam might teach in theory, it really comes down to what this particular guy is like, what his family is like, what strand of Islam they come from, how he's been influenced by growing up in Australia, what school he's gone to, who his friends are. I don't want to tell you your business, Mike, but maybe you just need to get to know the guy."

What happened next surprised Michael, I think, as much as me. He slammed his fist hard onto the arm of his chair.

"I don't want to get to know him! I just want him to stay away!"

The words were loud, and they hung in the air. Dylan looked up from his Duplo and started to cry.

"Oh great!" said Michael, and went to Dylan. "It's all right, it's all right." He took him in his arms and comforted him, but the howling didn't diminish in volume.

Then the doorbell rang.

"Could you get that for me?" Michael asked.

I wandered down the hall, pleased to escape from the noise which I regarded as being as much my fault as Michael's. There were two shapes outlined in the frosted glass of the front door, and as I opened it, I silently hoped it was not the Jehovah's Witnesses.

It wasn't. Two boys stood on the landing. They were in their late teens, big for their age, dressed in the uniform of their sub-culture (the ridiculously baggy jeans, the white t-shirts, the garish jackets). One of them I recognized as Kelly's boyfriend. He was the one who spoke.

"Is Michael there? Tell him it's Youseff. Tell him I want to talk to him."

I hesitated. I didn't like the possibilities that formed in my mind. The two of them both looked edgy, nervous. If Youseff only wanted to talk to Michael, why had he brought reinforcements? And the second boy was even bigger than Youseff. Media-driven images of gangs of knife-wielding youths of 'middle-Eastern descent' whirled through my mind.

I started to say, "Listen, I'm sorry, but Michael's not…" when I became aware of Michael standing behind me. He pushed past me onto the landing, and the two boys took a step back. There was just room for the three of them to stand there together, the two boys facing the middle-aged man, who (I was almost surprised to notice) was bigger than both of them.

"You've got a hide coming here. What makes you think I want to see you, let alone speak to you?" said Michael.

Youseff's eyes flashed. His voice was hard-edged. "Listen, I came here to try to talk to you, but I knew you wouldn't even try and listen." Youseff's voice was rising, and the sentences were coming faster. He jabbed the air with the finger of his right-hand as he spoke. "You're all the same. You hate us. You don't want us here. And you won't talk to me. So what's the point? At least Kelly talks to me."

Michael just stood there, and said nothing. I could see his right hand clenching and unclenching, and shaking slightly.

"What are you scared of anyway?" Youseff went on. "You worried that Daddy's little girl is going to get knocked up? Well you won't have to worry."

Youseff began to reach with his right hand into the inside pocket of his jacket, and Michael didn't wait to see what he was reaching for. He swung his right fist hard at Youseff's face. Youseff swayed back, and managed to avoid the punch, but not the left from Michael that followed it. It caught him flush on the cheek, and he staggered back, with his friend trying to hold him and Michael stepping forward ready to strike again. The two boys teetered for a moment on the top step, and then fell in a tangle of limbs down the three front steps, landing on the brick edging between the path and the small patch of lawn.

For what seemed like minutes there was only the sound of Michael breathing heavily, and the two boys groaning and swearing.

Youseff was the first to get to his feet. He looked shaken, and there was blood trickling down the side of his neck. He turned to Michael.

"Man, I don't know what your problem is. I only came to give you this."

He reached into his jacket pocket again and pulled out a crumpled piece of yellow paper, folded into four. He threw it towards Michael, and it fluttered unsteadily like the leaf from a particularly vivid tree, and landed on the top step.

"I didn't think you'd talk to me, so I wrote it down." Youseff helped his friend to his feet. "Come on, let's go."

And just like that they were gone, stumbling off down the street in the rain, looking darkly back over their shoulders at us, and talking together animatedly.

Michael stared at the piece of paper. He stepped forward and sat down on the top step, picking up the paper and slowly unfolding it. There were two sheets, with large handwriting on them.

From in the house, Dylan started to howl, but Michael didn't even turn his head. I quietly turned and walked back down the hall to comfort Dylan. Of course, when it was me that appeared in the doorway, and started to advance towards him, Dylan only howled louder and retreated beneath the coffee table.

10

IT WAS TWO DAYS later that I learnt from Michael the contents of Youseff's letter.

I had popped over to see if Michael wanted to continue our Islam chats, which were rapidly becoming chats about life, the universe, the nature of truth, the history of Western thought, and everything. I suspected that, like me, Michael hadn't imagined the conversation would go in quite the direction that it had.

It was after dinner, and Michael was out on the deck, with a cup of tea, gazing out into the quiet darkness of the backyard. He didn't see me emerge from the shadows until I was nearly at the back-steps, and he looked up with a start.

"Where did you come from?"

"Oh, I've been hiding behind the shed, hoping that Dylan would come and talk to me again." I flopped down into the chair beside him.

"I think you're on a lost cause there, mate. He's not talking to anyone much at the moment. Especially after the other day."

There was a brief silence, as 'the other day' hung in the air.

"Listen", I said, "I'm sorry about…"

Michael jumped in. "Don't be ridiculous. You haven't got anything to be sorry about. Unlike certain other people."

He gave a rueful snort. "I certainly managed to stuff that one up."

I tried to sound sympathetic. "Well, you shouldn't be too hard on yourself. You were under stress. A young Muslim guy winds you up, stands there looking threatening, and then reaches into his jacket. A lot of people would say that what you did was very understandable."

"Maybe", said Michael, "but then again maybe not. I mean, why didn't I want Kelly to go out with this guy? Because I don't trust Muslims. They're violent, right? Short-tempered. Volatile. Unlike me, of course!"

He shook his head ruefully, and stared into his cup. Silence hung in the air. In the end, my curiosity could wait no longer.

"And what was in the letter?"

"Well… that's the delicious irony, isn't it? He was writing to explain to me why he was breaking up with Kelly."

"Breaking up?"

"Yep. And it's basically because she isn't a Muslim, and he doesn't see any future in their relationship. He said that he likes her very much and all that, but that his family would never accept her, or allow him to marry her. She doesn't much believe in God, and certainly wouldn't be willing to wear the veil. And so he was writing to me because he thought that he owed me an explanation, as her father, as to why he wouldn't be seeing her any more."

"You're kidding."

"Not at all. It was a very earnest, serious letter."

"So how's Kelly taking it?"

"Well, she isn't speaking to me. It's all my fault of course, and Julie basically agrees. And Dylan starts crying every time I leave the room. So it's all fun over here, I can tell you."

Michael stared blankly out into the backyard.

"What about you? How are you feeling about it?"

"I don't know. Pretty stupid. Guilty, too, I guess. I mean, how would you feel?"

"The same I suppose…"

My voice trailed off, and there was silence for a while. I figured it was time to leave Michael alone with his misery, and that I could ask him about our Islam chats another time. I gave him a brotherly, sympathetic slap on the shoulder as I stood up, and headed home.

━━ ⊰◆⊱ ━━

Over the next couple of days, I sat at my desk trying to make sense of the drafts I'd written, with all the comments scribbled on them after my conversations with Michael. I felt there was something there—a book waiting to get out—but I wasn't sure at this stage what it was.

The strange thing was that in the midst of all these big thoughts about Islam, Western society, and our attitudes to religion, I kept coming back to Michael himself, and to what had happened with Youseff.

In the end, I put my piles of paper to one side.

Dear Michael

I've been sitting here for the last two days at my desk trying to work out where to go next with the 'Islam project'. I've enjoyed talking with you about it, and have found our conversations really useful in thinking about the material. In fact, I was going to ask you the other night whether you wanted to keep going—I think I have some more things to write about, but I'm not exactly sure what.

But in the meantime, as I've been sitting here trying to get my head around it, I can't stop thinking about what happened with Youseff.

So being someone who writes better than he talks (I think), I've decided to write to you. (And also because I think that what I want to say to you, if I try to do it in person, would probably come out all wrong.)

I know you're feeling lousy about it all, and I would be too, I think, in your circumstances. And I probably would have done much the same thing with the same provocation (if I could throw a left-hook like you, that is).

But it occurs to me that there is some good that can come out of what happened. And it's related to everything we've been discussing about Islam. I'll try to explain what I mean.

In the first few chapters that we discussed, we tried to wrap our minds around what Islam really was and is, at those things which unify it, and those things which indicate its great diversity. One of our constant questions was: Is Islam really violent and expansionist, in its core principles? I ended up answering a qualified yes to this, based on what the Qur'an and hadith literature actually say, and at

Islamic practice and law down the centuries. But I think it's a qualified yes; a yes-but. Even though Islam can be construed, legitimately enough, to provide a justification for militaristic expansion and violent resistance in the name of Allah, that by no means implies that the world's one billion Muslims are all bent on murdering Westerners in their beds. There are clearly a great many people in the world who own a Muslim identity who seem to have no wish whatsoever to go down the path of violence.

Which raises an interesting question: Given the provocation, given the circumstances, given the opportunity, would a great many more Muslims (including those living in the West) rise up and fight in the name of Allah? Would they be ready to do violence to protect themselves, or to achieve their goals?

The answer to that is found simply by looking in the mirror. Islam is a vehicle for violence and aggression for precisely the reason that the human heart is so commonly violent and aggressive. In other words, perhaps we are looking for something in the actions of the September 11 terrorists that we should equally expect to find buried somewhere in our psyches. The desire to lash out at those we blame for our troubles, the tendency to rationalise the harm we do to others in the pursuit of what we see as our legitimate rights, the obsession with our own freedom and happiness that obliterates our respect for others and their desire for the same, the willingness to do violence (emotional, verbal, physical) to break down any barriers that stand between me and my desires.

I don't want to suggest that there's a moral equivalence between your punching a young Muslim, and September

11. There isn't. What I am saying is that the big problems we've been discussing also have a personal dimension.

And it is this: how do I understand, and deal with, the obvious fact of my own moral imperfection, my own inability to live even according to the somewhat lowered standards I've set for myself? In your case, the impulse to violence that smashes a young kid in the face because he wanted to talk to you. In my case, and everyone else's case, a thousand ways in which we selfishly say and do what suits us, even if it is damaging to other people.

It's a problem that we *all* share, whether we're Muslims, Christians or something else.

Speaking personally, this is one of the main reasons I find Christianity so persuasive: it not only affirms the fact of human selfishness and immorality ('sin' as it's called); it also provides a solution. I don't know how much you remember from that Sunday School your Methodist grandma sent you to, but this is where the death of Christ comes in. Christ's death as an act of atonement is the means by which God deals with the problem of our constant failure to be moral (our selfishness, our violence, our lying, our anger, and so on). It's the door to forgiveness.

I guess, thinking back over what I've been writing about Islam, the death of Christ looms very large. The denial of his death by the Qur'an is a terrible blunder, it seems to me. At one level, it's a blunder because it casts so much doubt on the veracity or reliability of the Qur'anic statements. If it can be so wrong historically at this point, it doesn't do much for our confidence in the revelation as a whole.

But it's tragic at another level as well. In denying the

fundamental teaching of Christianity—that Christ died for our sins—Islam leaves itself locked up in a world with a holy, pure God, and very ordinary, sinful people, but no just and reasonable way for the two to be reconciled. It's the problem of justice and mercy that we talked about at one point. How can Allah be all-just and yet all-merciful at the same time? That's what the cross does in Christian thought—it's the means by which the utterly moral God remains moral, and yet forgives immoral people. He deals with the punishment himself, in pouring it out on his own Son, so that guilty people (like me) can be forgiven.

Like so many before and since, Muhammad found the cross offensive. No prophet of God could die such a humiliating death, he reasoned. It surely could not be God's plan to see such a holy man crucified. And so it could never have happened.

People find it offensive today for different reasons. It seems passé, old-fashioned, barbarous, irrelevant—whatever. But that it might be true, and that it might be the answer, we don't stop to consider.

The other night, Michael, when you said you felt guilty about Youseff, I came out with the usual platitudes about not being too hard on yourself, and how it was very understandable, and all that. It's the kind of thing you say. But it was a stupid thing to say. Of course it's right to feel bad about what you did, to feel guilty. In fact, what sort of guy would you be if you didn't feel some guilt about what you did?

What I want to say to you is that the cross of Christ has an answer to guilt that I don't think you'll find anywhere else. It's an answer you might not have thought about for a long while, if ever. But I wouldn't be much of a friend if I didn't point you in that direction, because I have certainly found it to be an immensely satisfying answer and—I have to say this in light of our discussion—a true one.

I don't know what you think about all this, Michael. But the more I think about it, the more sure I am that the challenge of Islam for us as Westerners is to reconsider why we've abandoned our Christian heritage—not only in the big social sense, but also personally. Because in abandoning it (without adequate reason in my view) we find ourselves in a terrible mess, intellectually and morally.

I'm hoping that your response to all this will *not* be some relativist cop-out—'Oh it might be true for you, but that's just your opinion'. I'd prefer you to come back to me and say, 'Well thanks for the thoughts, but I could never be a Christian, because I just don't think it is *true*. And here's why...'

I would love you to say that, because that's a conversation worth having; it's a discussion worth spending a few more Monday afternoons on.

On that scary, but hopeful note, I'll sign off. Thanks again for helping me out over the past several weeks. I don't know what it's been like for you, but I've enjoyed it.

See you in the backyard.

T.

ALSO AVAILABLE
FROM
THE GOOD BOOK
COMPANY...

A Fresh Start

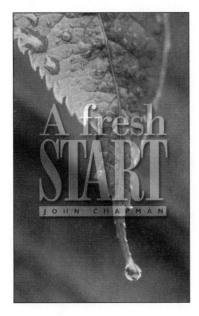

John Chapman's clear, persuasive and engaging presentation of the good news of Jesus is as fresh and readable as ever. The book gives a straightforward explanation of our problem before God, his solution, how we can know it is all true, and what we should do about it.

Highly recommended.

Jesus on Trial

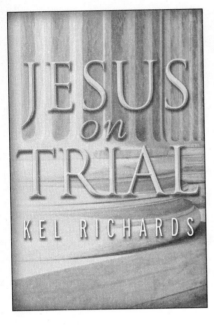

Popular author and radio commentator Kel Richards presents the evidence for Jesus' resurrection in a fresh and compelling way. Taking the analogy of a court case, *Jesus on Trial* demonstrates that the evidence for the resurrection satisfies our requirements of truth. The reader is in the position of juror, and is challenged to make a decision on the evidence as it is presented clearly and plainly by Kel. The appealing format and clear, simple writing makes this an easy book to give away to enquiring or sceptical friends.

Ordering details:

The Good Book Company
Telephone: 0845 225 0880
Facsimile: 0845 225 0990
Email: admin@thegoodbook.co.uk

www.thegoodbook.co.uk

PURE SEX

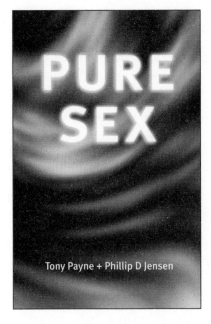

Tony Payne + Phillip D Jensen

Phillip Jensen and Tony Payne take a look at what the Bible teaches about sex, and at what this means in the sexual climate of the new millennium. In doing so, they give Christians clear and compelling reasons for standing apart and being different from the world around them; but they also provide a challenge to the non-Christian person who realises that something is very wrong with the model of sexuality we are now living with after the sexual revolution.

This compelling book shows how our society has come to hold such a confused and destructive view of sex, and why the Bible's alternative is so liberating.

ORDERING DETAILS:

The Good Book Company
Telephone: 0845 225 0880
Facsimile: 0845 225 0990
Email: admin@thegoodbook.co.uk

www.thegoodbook.co.uk

THE ESSENCE OF DARWINISM

Is Darwinism true? Is it the only theory that can explain our origins? Should we care? Are we taking Genesis seriously enough?

In her fourth book in *The Essence of* series, Dr Kirsten Birkett considers these frequently asked questions. In an area in which there seem to be so many conflicting answers, she takes a fresh look at the controversy by getting behind the surface disputes to look at what is really being argued over. At the same time, this book provides a compact and accessible summary of the important points of the Darwinian theory so far.

The Essence of Darwinism is an easy-to-read book for all thinkers from senior high school onwards.

ORDERING DETAILS:

The Good Book Company
Telephone: 0845 225 0880
Facsimile: 0845 225 0990
Email: admin@thegoodbook.co.uk

www.thegoodbook.co.uk

Simply Christianity: Beyond Religion

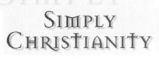

Simply Christianity

Beyond Religion

John Dickson

One of the reasons people sometimes avoid looking into Christianity is that there are so many versions on offer, each with its own religious package. The project of this book is to get beyond the rituals, myth and dogma. By going back to the earliest biographies of Jesus— the Gospels in the New Testament—*Simply Christianity* finds what remains after the 'religion' is stripped away. It's a great book for understanding the core of Christian faith.

Ordering details:

The Good Book Company
Telephone: 0845 225 0880
Facsimile: 0845 225 0990
Email: admin@thegoodbook.co.uk

www.thegoodbook.co.uk